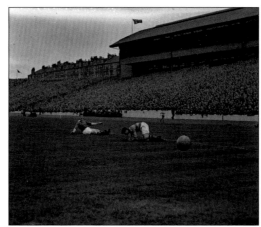

To purchase any of the photos in this book, printed up, in a selection of sizes, go to:

www.photoshopscotland.co.uk

For a 10% discount on all orders enter RANGERS at checkout

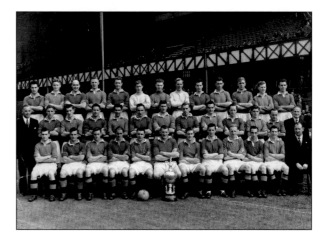

RANGERS
IN THE BLACK & WHITE ERA

By Steve Finan

ISBN 978-1-84535-844-0

First published in Great Britain in 2020 by DC Thomson & Co., Ltd., Meadowside, Dundee, DD1 9QJ

To purchase this book visit **www.dcthomsonshop.co.uk**

Or Freephone 0800 318 846 / Overseas customers call +44 1382 575580

Typeset & internal design by Steve Finan.

COVER/BACK COVER DESIGN | LEON STRACHAN

In compiling this book my thanks go to:

Leon Strachan.	Connor Vearnals.	Nikki Fleming.	Gary Thomas.
David Walker.	Julie-Ann Marshall.	Deirdre Vincent.	Duncan Laird.
James Kirk.	Gill Martin.	Craig Houston.	Brian Wright.
Jim Wilson.	Sylwia Jackowska.	David Powell.	Lewis Finan.
Mindy Lynch.	Jacqui Hunter.	Barry Sullivan.	Fraser T. Ogilvie.

Introduction

RANGERS Football Club has a history that makes it the greatest, the most trophy-laden, club in the world. Rangers, starting in the black and white era, became the measure that all other clubs strived to live up to.

All of the photographs in this book were taken in those great days, but have been hidden for decades.

The Rangers have a rightness, a worth, a properness about them that has been building for six or seven generations. Indeed, since Moses was a boy.

There was a collective mind-set among those who made Rangers what Rangers must be, much of it founded upon the ideals laid down by Mr William Wilton, then Mr William Struth after him. Second best wasn't nearly good enough. Even winning by a narrow margin wasn't good enough. Rangers Football Club became a dreadnought that carried all before it. Any opposition was outgunned, any show of defiance was met with a display of power.

The players who became known as "Rangers greats" were a breed apart. Any player who considered himself a Rangers player had to ask: am I one of the weak or one of the strong? There could be only one way to answer. Rangers are the strong. Rangers are the strongest.

The above is an attempt to explain the ethos of Rangers, and what it meant to be a Rangers man in the black and white era.

But words can only take you so far. This book sets out to show what those words mean.

You will have seen many old Rangers photos. This book, however, shows photos that (mostly) haven't previously been published. They have lain in archives for 50, 60 or 70 years. Some were taken for newspapers or magazines, but many were never even developed from negatives. They remained in that state until someone came along looking for them.

Some of the photographs are damaged. They are old and brittle. A few negatives picked up blemishes from exposure to light.

I could have had them digitally repaired, as photos can be manipulated so cleverly these days. But I resisted all entreaties from page design artists to do so. I felt it more honest to present the photos as they are – genuine historical artefacts, if a little tattered round the edges.

Some of the photos are from the personal moments of Rangers men. Half a century ago, press photographers enjoyed much more access to players' private lives than today. These photos have a charm and an interest all of their own.

Above all, these images will, I hope, evoke nostalgia. These are the players you grew up watching, or the players your father and grandfather saw. If even one photo makes you say, "I was there, I remember him, I remember Ibrox like that", then I'll have done my job.

The time-frame I chose to call "the black & white era" is the distant past up to the late 1970s/early '80s.

There are tens of thousands of photos in the DC Thomson archive. I could have filled this book several times over. Choosing which to leave out was a painful process.

The Souness revolution and Walter Smith years deserve a book of photos to themselves – and I'll do that book soon.

There were many other photos I could have used, but chose not to because I judged them to have been widely seen in the past, in various places and books.

The aim of this book is to show what it was to follow The Rangers, be a Ranger, and understand The Rangers in the black and white era.

Lastly, this is not a definitive history of Rangers, nor does it pretend to be. There are many gaps. I apologise for that. There are players who deserve to be better celebrated, and games which might have been mentioned but are not. I only had 320 pages!

Steve Finan, 2020.

■ **Right: 1979: Derek Johnstone and Sandy Jardine stride across the crest mosaic (that adorns the cover of this book) at the Ibrox main entrance.**

CONTENTS

The Iron Curtain

THE most effective football unit to ever play in Scotland is a good place to start any book.

Winston Churchill's description of a geopolitical divide across Europe, with Soviet Russia's satellite states erecting an impenetrable border across the continent, was made on March 5th, 1946, at Westminster College, Missouri. His clever metaphor caught the world's attention and defined East-West relations for a couple of generations.

Or, at least, it defined Soviet-Western machinations everywhere except Glasgow. If you'd asked any football supporter in Govan what the Iron Curtain was, he'd tell you to take a walk down Helen Street or the Broomloan Road towards Ibrox Park.

In the years following the war, the Rangers defence was made up of a formidable, athletic, assured, and highly effective group of footballers. The classic line-up was: Bobby Brown in goal, George Young and Jock Shaw at full-back, Willie Woodburn at centre-half, and wing-halfs Ian McColl and Sammy Cox.

The 1950s was a golden era in Scottish football. A high-scoring era, and Rangers certainly scored a lot of goals themselves. But to be reliably solid at the back was the foundation of a great deal of success for the club.

And they had to be good. A telling measure of any football team can be taken by looking at the opposition they faced and defeated. This was the era of the Hibs Famous Five forward line, Smith, Johnstone, Reilly, Turnbull and Ormond, and the Terrible Trio of Bauld, Wardhaugh and Conn at Hearts. There was a resurgent and high-scoring Motherwell team under George Stevenson, and a formidable, trophy-winning Aberdeen under Dave Halliday.

These were all-time-great teams of their respective clubs, but all were blunted by the Iron Curtain.

A powerful defence is a Rangers tradition and these men are Ibrox legends.

There is an enduring myth that The Iron Curtain was mainly a physical force. But if you think that, then you don't know football. Each man was a ferocious tackler, it is true, but it takes skill and timing, as well as strength, to tackle properly. It takes more than strength to be a good footballer.

Bobby Brown was a gifted shot-stopper who dominated his box. The full-backs were good distributors when they had the time, robust and fast when it was called for. Willie Woodburn was the pivot, the rock in the centre, while McColl and Cox took care of the opposition inside-forwards, but were also very good passers of a ball, superb all-round footballers, and the base from which Rangers attacks were often mounted.

It is a tragedy that so little footage remains of this defensive system, as it would serve as a fine educational blueprint for players even today.

■ The curtain draws shut. Willie Woodburn stands ready as Bobby Brown confidently takes a high cross.

BETWEEN them, the six men most commonly recognised as "The Iron Curtain" (Brown, Woodburn, Shaw, McColl, Young and Cox) played a quite incredible 3169 times for Rangers. In the 1948-49 "triple crown" season they played 175 games out of a possible collective 180 that a 30-game League season allows. The following season they managed an incredible 178 games. Only Jock Shaw and Willie Woodburn missed a game apiece.

But why were they so effective?

Partly, as is shown from the stats, they were all very experienced players and almost superhumanly durable. Their goals-against tallies prove how consistent they were. In the eight league seasons (each a 30-game card) following the war:

1946-47 — 26 conceded. **1947-48** — 20 conceded.
1948-49 — 32 conceded. **1949-50** — 26 conceded.
1950-51 — 37 conceded. **1951-52** — 31 conceded.
1952-53 — 39 conceded. **1953-54** — 35 conceded.

The real secret, though, was teamwork. They knew how each other played, knew where each other would be, and knew how to cover when danger threatened. There was a superb discipline in their collective on-field positions.

Woodburn was the fulcrum, the world's best centre-half at this time. Sadly, when he is remembered it is the sine die ban (next page) that is talked of. But thinking of him only as a hard man is a disservice. He was superb in the air, continually getting to crosses (wingers feeding centre-forwards from the byline being a staple form of attack in this era.) Any trainer would tell his centre-forward to attack crosses in front of his marker. But Woodburn attacked crosses with better timing than most forwards. And it was rare for a centre-forward to "get across" a player who had such good anticipation.

He was also a commanding presence, urging co-defenders to greater efforts and giving them an angry blast whenever a goal was conceded. Add to that his two-footed distribution and his superb athletic balance (his running style was a thing of beauty) and it should be apparent that this was a Rolls-Royce of a defender.

■ Willie Woodburn characteristically getting to a ball ahead of the striker in a Scotland-Wales Home International. Note the superbly-balanced, in control Woodburn, compared to a Welshman hastily attempting to change direction.

IT is tempting to look at the decision to ban Willie Woodburn from football "sine die" (Latin for "no future date designated" – so for all time) through modern eyes. Players rack up dozens of red cards these days and no one seems to bat an eye.

But, even for the time, the Woodburn ban was a ridiculous over-reaction. He had been sent off three times in his career before the game against Stirling Albion on August 28th, 1954, a League Cup tie at Ibrox.

In the last minute of the game, with Rangers winning 2-0, Willie became involved with Stirling's inside-right Alex Paterson.

Willie had been playing with an injury and was severely provoked by incidents in the game.

He was summoned to appear before the Referees Committee, who handled disciplinary matters in those days.

Rumours flew around Scottish football that an example was to be made and a six-month ban was being considered. Willie, just past his 35th birthday, had privately said that if the

■ September 14th, 1954. Willie and manager Scot Symon emerge from the referee's committee hearing, having just heard the life sentence being passed.

ban was of such a length, he would probably give up playing.

However, the committee gave Woodburn a hearing that lasted all of four minutes, then handed down their sentence. There has never been a sine die ban of such a high-profile player in Scottish football since that day.

Willie, known as Big Ben, certainly wasn't an angel. No defender in those days was.

He was a fierce competitor, and didn't let anyone take liberties with him, or his team-mates.

Though Rangers didn't appeal the decision, the feeling behind the scenes was one of astonishment at the harshness of the ban. Woodburn had given sterling service to Scotland and was, in any case, in the late twilight of his career.

Willie had an interest in a successful motor business (and would go on to be a journalist) but the committee also robbed him of his football wages and any continuing livelihood in the game because the terms of the ban prohibited him from being a coach or a manager, not just a player.

The ban was lifted in 1957, and Willie was posthumously (he died in 2001) inducted into the Scottish Football Hall of Fame in 2004.

Far too little, far too late.

■ Tiger Shaw, left, in the blue and white hooped shirt Rangers wore as a change top in the late 1940s. Such a strip had also been used, with wider hoops, in 1907 and in the 1930s. See also page 156.

Full-back play was different in the late-1940s/early 1950s to what it is today. With a defence playing just one centre-half, full-backs were deployed solely as defenders. There wasn't the space or opportunity to be an overlapping full-back, or wing-back, as is understood today. Full-backs were there to counter wingers, or outside-forwards. The job was to stop crosses coming into the box.

Tiger Shaw was a defender to the core of his being. A tough man, of course, but it takes more than that to be a good defender. Shaw timed his tackles superbly well and was fit and fast, with lightning-quick reactions.

Incredibly, he played for Rangers until he was 42, though more rarely in his final few seasons.

If only the club had been able to distil the essence of the Tiger into a bottle of elixir to sprinkle over all those who would ever don the Rangers colours.

■ Right: Tiger, as captain, leads out The Rangers for the 1946 Southern League Cup Final.

■ George Young was the most charismatic Scottish footballer of the immediate post-war period. The badly damaged photo above (a mock-up, an early attempt at what a newspaper today would term an "infographic") was to illustrate his impressive penalty-taking technique. George would happily go along with such stunts, cracking jokes, taking the mickey, as he did so. There weren't many personalities as big as George.

■ George captaining Scotland v. France in Paris on May 27th, 1950.

GEORGE LEWIS YOUNG, Rangers 1941-57, is one of the most famous names in even Rangers' storied history. He was a giant of a presence in the Scottish game in every sense.

A natural centre-half, he moved to right-back to accommodate the presence of Willie Woodburn, though moved back again after Woodburn's suspension.

George was 6 feet, 2 inches and weighed 15 stone, but looked even bigger. Indeed, in the large-shouldered suits of the 1940s and '50s, and with his barrel-chested physique, he was a massively imposing figure even when not on the pitch.

He was powerful, very good in the air, and a redoubtable defender. He was also a very fair player. Stories abound of his sportsmanship, and even of him encouraging and calming the nerves of debutant opposition strikers by talking to them on the pitch.

Though a defender, he was the instigator of many a Rangers goal. George's prodigious strength allowed him to fire a ball 70 yards, turning defence to attack. Rangers profited enormously from this, with Young sending an accurate long ball to Thornton at inside-forward, or Waddell at outside-right, being an enduring feature of their play in the 1950s.

Kicking a ball that distance might not sound too impressive nowadays. But it was highly unusual with an old leather tub on a wet day when it could double in weight by absorbing water.

George was captain of Scotland and gained 54 caps, the first Scot to amass more than 50, as well as playing in a further 22 Scottish League games. Indeed, in the days before a national team manager George was trusted to organise the Scotland team. He would make the team's travel plans, arrange cinema visits during away trips, and even conduct training.

To the ire of some players, George also had a big say in team selection. Indeed, when it was suggested to Sir George Graham, secretary of the Scottish Football Association, that Scotland might employ a team manager in the same way England had appointed Walter Winterbottom, Graham replied, "We don't need a manager. We've got George."

However, quite apart from his prowess as a footballer and an organiser, George Young was an engaging, charismatic figure. A natural leader of men, he commanded respect from all around him.

There was many a rumour that he would one day be Rangers manager, but the timing was never right and sadly it didn't happen.

Even before he retired as a player in 1957, George ran a restaurant and coffee bar in Glasgow's Union Street and owned the Tillietudlem Hotel in Crossford. It was a world he was comfortable in, being a genial and popular host.

He was manager of Third Lanark for a few years and sat on the pools panel in the early sixties.

Everyone liked George Young. He was a great ambassador for Rangers, a colossus, a gentleman, and deservedly the first man to be inducted into the Scottish Football Hall of Fame.

■ **Many a fleet-footed winger thought he'd got past George Young.**

But, as shown here, George was adept at getting in a tackle when it seemed too late. One of those long legs would snake out to prod the ball to safety

Though he is remembered as a genial giant, and a very decent bloke, George's effectiveness as a defender should not be overlooked.

It took the Rangers defence quite some time to recover after he retired at the end of the 1956-57 season.

They missed not only his abilities as a footballer, but his massive on-field presence.

■ **Bobby Brown was an excellent goalkeeper, and a very intelligent man.**

He was capped for Scotland while still an amateur at Queen's Park and remained a part-timer throughout his Rangers career, being a PE teacher at Denny High School.

He replaced fans' favourite from before the war, Jerry Dawson, so had to be good to satisfy the Ibrox crowd.

Bobby became a fixture in the Iron Curtain defence, however, his blond curls earning him the nickname of "the golden boy". He once played 179 successive games.

He went on to become St Johnstone manager for nine years, then the first proper manager of Scotland in 1967 when the old selection committee method of choosing the team was abandoned.

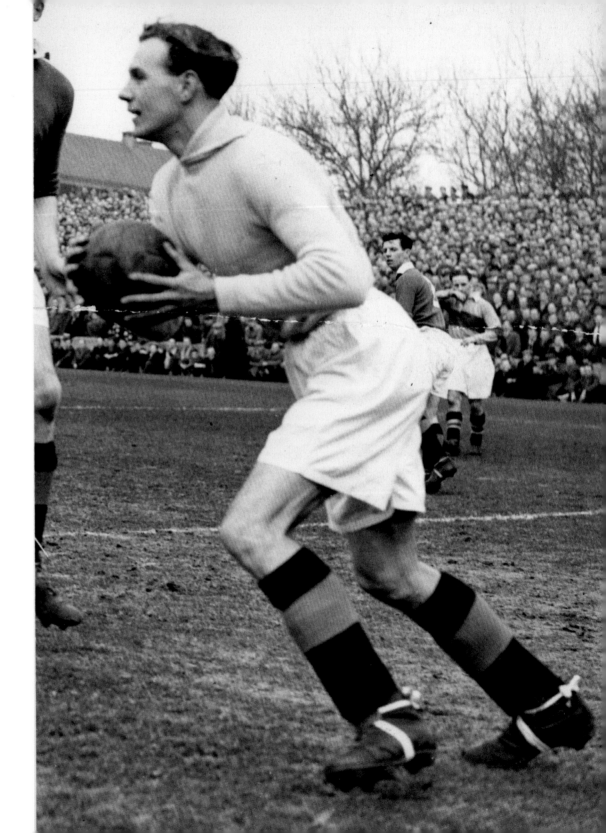

■ **Ian McColl spent 15 seasons with Rangers, playing 575 competitive games and lifting 13 major trophies.**

He was strong, tall, and always fully committed. A winner to his core. The archetypal Rangers attitude.

He played from 1946 to 1961, the last of the Iron Curtain men to retire. He was a half-back and you could count the number of 50-50 tackles he lost on the fingers of one hand.

Before the term was ever coined, McColl was a midfield enforcer. You didn't make compromises in the Rangers half-back line, because a compromise wasn't a win.

But he could play a bit too, he was a gifted passer.

Ian McColl was the sort of player that supporters love. The man who it is plain to see is playing for the shirt, hates to lose, runs his heart out, gives all he can in every game, and yet has game-changing skill.

■ SAMMY COX. What a player. Great athlete, great skill, great attitude.

He was one of those players who looked like a veteran from his very first game. He was good at everything, and could have filled several positions.

But Sammy was another who had his career badly interrupted by the war. He didn't make his Rangers debut until he was 26, but went on to give a decade of excellent service.

It isn't every player you could have looked at back then and thought that he'd still be a superstar today. But Cox is one such. His energy, unfailing ability to find a man with his passes, sharp tackling, and energetic athleticism would have won him a place in even the most celebrated modern teams. Sammy could have played in the Brazil side of 1970, a Dutch team alongside Cruyff, or Guardiola's Barcelona.

He could do absolutely everything a footballer needs to do – instantly control a ball, then just as quickly turn out of danger to find a pass. Add to that his impeccable positioning, his sixth sense to danger, and his footballing intelligence, and you begin to get a picture of just how valuable a player Sammy was.

Every team would benefit from having a Sammy Cox in the engine room.

■ **Willie Thornton in 1951.**

It must be acknowledged, of course, that the rest of that post-war "Iron Curtain" team were very good players too.

The winning of League championships may need a firm defence, but it is the forwards who build the victories atop the solid foundation.

Willie Thornton played a huge role in the overall success of the team. He was a prolific scorer – one of the best headers of a ball the Scottish game has ever seen.

He was also a polite, genial, and very sporting man.

Willie spent his entire playing career with Rangers, before going on to be manager of Dundee, then Partick, before returning to Ibrox as assistant to Davie White in 1968. He was kept on in the role by Willie Waddell.

Aye, Willie Thornton could play a bit.

Mr Struth

IN the modern world, studies would be made of a record of sustained high achievement such as the one Mr William Struth kept in place for 34 years.

There would be analysis of his methods, university courses studying him, and he'd barely be able to get into his office for TV documentary crews. They'd all be clamouring to learn the secret of that continual success.

What they would find, and what would be looked at most closely, would nowadays be called the "workplace culture" Mr Struth created at Ibrox. Because if there is a secret to his success, that is it.

Mr Struth's oft-repeated tenet that "only the best is good enough for The Rangers" perfectly sums it up. He demanded the very best treatment for his men, the best clothes, the best travel arrangements, the best of everything. And this rubbed off on his players.

They were made to feel like the elite, so they played like the elite.

All of Mr Struth's famous rules added to this feeling. Making sure the turns on all the players socks were of the same depth; making sure their sleeves were rolled up to a uniform length; insisting that players put their shorts on last so they didn't risk going out on to the park with creases; insisting on made-to-measure suits, bowler hats, round toe-capped shoes. It was psychology. It made his players look the best and then play better than the rest.

It sounds simple, doesn't it. So why didn't every other team adopt similar standards? For one thing, though tales of how Mr Struth ran Rangers are common knowledge now, they weren't widely known during his term of office. The days when newspapers or football reporters would reveal and analyse managerial techniques in this way were still many years off.

In any case, to properly enforce such rules required a quite remarkable strength of personality. If just one maverick player had decided he was going to wear his shirt outside his socks, or walked with his hands in his pockets, then the aura of discipline would be cracked.

But none did. Or if they tried, they didn't last long. There were many big personalities in the dressing room of Struth's Rangers – the likes of David Meiklejohn, Alan Morton, Dougie Gray, and Bob McPhail. But none with a strength of will, or desire, to defy the boss.

It is a great shame that more of Mr Struth's methods weren't captured on film. Today, though his place in the pantheon of world football legends is assured, his personality and manner of speaking are almost unknown. Very little footage of him exists.

A century has passed since Mr Struth became manager of The Rangers. In centuries to come, his name will still be revered.

■ **Rangers captain George Young at the Ibrox reception for Mr Struth's retirement in 1954.**

28

■ **Left:** Mr Struth would be driven around Glasgow looking at potential signings. Sometimes he trusted his Rangers to play at Ibrox, and win, while he attended a game elsewhere.

The car is a piece of Rangers history. It was a 1933 Austin 12, registration US 3322, owned and driven by Tom Petrie. The chassis was strong enough, Tom would proudly claim, to carry two full Rangers team hampers in the boot.

Tom started helping out Mr Struth during the petrol rationing years and carried on as Rangers' driver into the 1960s.

■ **Right:** A retirement toast to Mr Struth in the Ibrox boardroom on the evening of Thursday, May 6th, 1954. Glasgow Provost Thomas Kerr, Rangers skipper George Young, and Rangers chairman, Bailie John F. Wilson, raise a glass to the great man.

■ The annual "Sports", athletics meetings at Ibrox, were a great favourite of Mr Struth, who was a talented runner in his youth and a highly effective athletics coach

The event was a matter of personal pride to him, and attracted crowds of between 40,000 and 50,000.

Athletes such as Paavo Nurmi, the great Finnish middle and long-distance runner appeared, as did the celebrated Eric Liddell of *Chariots of Fire* fame.

Alfie Shrubb (a world-famous athlete of his day) set seven world records for middle to long-distance running in the early 20th Century on what was regarded as the excellent track surface at Ibrox.

Mr Struth regularly travelled to London and even America to recruit athletes to take part.

The Sports continued until the mid-1960s.

■ Mr Struth at The Ibrox Sports.

■ Mr Struth with his great friend Paddy Travers, who at this point was the manager of a very successful Clyde team. Mr Struth would take holidays on the Isle of Man with Paddy, a former Celtic player.

■ **Mr Struth kept a greenhouse behind the Broomloan Road end of Ibrox. It is testament to the respect he commanded that it was never once vandalised by visiting supporters.**

■ **Mr Struth was very successful runner, making a living from his professional races at Highland Games or other track meetings.**

It was a very popular sport at the turn of the 19th to 20th Century, drawing large crowds.

In those days, racers were handicapped a few yards, depending on how they had performed in previous races. So often winning just made it more difficult in subsequent races.

It was his supreme fitness, and ability to pass on his methods to footballers (who weren't so fit in those days) that got him the trainer's job at Clyde in 1908, which in turn led to him being recruited as trainer at Ibrox in 1914.

He became manager on May 20th, 1920, and remained in the post for 34 years, 26 days. He stepped down on June 15th, 1954.

He adhered to high standards himself, of course, even after having a leg amputated in 1950.

It is testament to Mr Struth that his name, his strength of character, and the standards of behaviour he insisted upon, are still talked of at Ibrox today.

The modern Rangers are built upon his ideals.

■ **Mr Struth in 1920.**

■ **On May 15th, 1953, the city of Glasgow presented Mr Struth with a portrait in oils (right), which to this day hangs in the Ibrox trophy room.**

It was following that special lunch that he gave the speech which is most associated with him, in which he said, "To be a Ranger is to sense the sacred trust of upholding all that such a name means in this shrine of football . . . No true Ranger has ever failed in the tradition set him."

When Mr Struth formally retired the players and directors presented him with a TV-radiogram before heading off – without him for the first time in 34 years – on the tour of Canada that is depicted on page 98.

He died at his imposing sandstone home in Dalkeith Avenue, Dumbreck, on September 21st, 1956, the day before the first Old Firm match of the 1956-57 season. Rangers won 2-0.

At his funeral a few days later Sammy Baird, John Little, Ian McColl, George Niven, Willie Rae, and George Young carried him to his final resting place at Craigton Cemetery, not far from Ibrox.

■ **This photo of Mr Struth's oil painting was taken in 1959, and is being examined here by Rangers chairman Bailie John F. Wilson. The portrait is still there, but there are now many more league championship flags to accompany it.**

■ **The last word on Mr Struth will go to someone who knew him well, but who didn't enjoy the acceptance or tolerance that came from being one of his players.**

It is an account by a newspaper reporter signing himself The Traveller, from 1952, written when rumours first began to circulate that the seemingly immortal Boss might actually one day retire.

Many legends, anecdotes and quotes, by and about Mr Struth, have emerged in the years since. So this should be read from the point of view of when it was written – when Mr Struth was a very private man who kept his methods and Ibrox business more private still. He was a mysterious, deity-like figure to the ordinary fan.

This was a candid piece of writing for its respectful-of-authority times. Newspapers didn't often do articles like this, that reported feelings and impressions instead of facts. Indeed, it is possible the writer was never allowed to enter Ibrox again!

The Man Who Lives For Rangers . . .

YOU stand before a closed, panelled door at the top of a blue and white tiled stairway. The one frosted pane of glass in front of you is simply inscribed "Manager."

You knock. A small sign lights up at the right of the door. "Engaged," it says, if you're out of luck. But this time you're O.K. "Enter," says the sign, and in you go.

A dry husky monotone greets you— "Good day. What can I do for you? And it's advisable to have your answer ready. For this is the sanctum of Mr William Struth, J.P., vice-chairman and manager of Rangers. And Mr Struth is no man for idle gossip—as you'll gather if you have time to note the light-blue notice on the wall, which says, "Brief, I pray you, for you see.

Ever since he joined the club, Bill Struth has lived for Rangers. To him, Ibrox Park is home.

He lunches there. After lunch he has a nap on the couch in his office. Any callers are told, "Nobody allowed up till three o'clock." And that means NOBODY!

But once you've been in, you marvel at the smartness and vitality of the

BY THE TRAVELLER

man who looks so much more like Mr William Struth, J.P., than Bill Struth, football manager. Which is just how you are intended to think. for Rangers' chief is a great believer in applied psychology, in putting over the Ibrox tradition of superiority.

Once upon a time, Bill Struth summoned to his office a young player who'd just arrived at Ibrox.

"Now you're a Rangers player," he told the youngster, "you have to keep to a high standard in everything you do. Not only in your behaviour on the field, but also when you leave Ibrox Park.

"You are being well-paid, so dress well. If you go to the theatre, take the best seats. As a Ranger you will be noticed everywhere you go. You — and the club—will be judged as people find you.

That is the policy he, himself, has followed through the years. A policy that has played a large part in making "Glasgow Rangers" one of the greatest names in football.

It is the first lesson the new Ibrox manager will have to learn when "The Old Man" finally retires from the scene.

YOU stand before a close panelled door at the top a blue and white tiled stairway. The one frosted pane of glass in front of you is simply inscribed "Manager".

You knock. A small sign lights at the right of the door. "Engaged" it says, if you're out of luck. But this time you're OK. "Enter" says the sign, and in you go.

A dry, husky monotone greets you. "Good day. What can I do for you?" And it's advisable to have your answer ready. For this is the sanctum of Mr William Struth JP, vice-chairman and manager of Rangers.

And Mr Struth is no man for idle gossip – you'll gather, if you have time to notice, the light-blue sign on the wall. It says. "Brief, I pray you. For you see it is a busy time with me. – Shakespeare."

Right away you get an impression of the personality of the man who has been boss of Ibrox for the past 32 years, and whose reported imminent retiral has been the talk of football these past few days.

He has long been a legendary figure in the game, this austere, clean-cut, silvery-haired man of 77.

"Mr Rangers" they've called him. And "Mr Football".

His record has been astonishing. Season after season, he has led Rangers to success after success. 18 Scottish League Championships, 10 Scottish Cup wins. Countless other honours.

And yet how little the man in the street really knows of him. Much of his character you may read in Ibrox Stadium itself, a wonderful monument to a remarkable man.

As you go through the swing doors into the main hall. Immediately comes the impression of dignity, aloofness, conscious superiority. You mount an imposing stairway which hammers home the impression. By the time you reach the manager's door you're feeling very modest, to say the least.

You can appreciate the psychological effect on any disgruntled player who seeks to put an imagined grievance before "The Boss".

Ask him a straight question and you'll get a straight answer. Ask him anything he doesn't think you should know, or he doesn't want to tell you, and you'll be told firmly, "That is the club's private business."

After a defeat which has shaken the football world into thoughts of a Rangers decline, he's liable to make some such pronouncement as: "defeat should be a spur to greater endeavour. After all, uninterrupted success can have its delusions."

Ever since he joined the club, Bill Struth has lived for Rangers.

To him, lbrox Park is home. He lunches there. After lunch he has a nap on the couch in his office.

Any callers are told, "Nobody allowed up till three o'clock." And that means NOBODY!

But once you've been in, you marvel at the smartness and vitality of the man who looks so much more like Mr William Struth J.P. than Bill Struth, football manager. Which is just how you are intended to think, for Rangers' chief is a great believer in applied psychology, in putting over the Ibrox tradition of superiority.

Once upon a time, Bill Struth summoned to his office a young player who'd just arrived at Ibrox.

"Now you're a Rangers player," he told the youngster, "you have to keep to a high standard in everything you do. Not only in your behaviour on the field, but also when you leave Ibrox Park. You are being well paid, so dress well. If you go to the theatre, take the best seats. As a Ranger you will be noticed everywhere you go. You – and the club – will be judged as people find you."

That is the policy he himself, has followed through the years. A policy that has played a large part in making Glasgow Rangers one of the greatest names in football.

It is the first lesson the new Ibrox manager will have to learn when "The Old Man" finally retires from the scene.

In his footsteps

IT was no easy thing to follow in the footsteps of Mr Struth in 1954 and become only the third manager of The Rangers. The task fell to former player Scot Symon, who was selected by his predecessor as "the one man who could do the job".

Symon had been East Fife's most successful manager and had just taken Preston North End to an FA Cup Final.

And it was a very difficult job he took at Rangers. He inherited an ageing squad (though there were some fine players coming through) and the challenge from other clubs has never been stronger than in the 1950s and 60s. In the 15 years, 1950 to 1965, seven clubs won the league and there were eight different winners of The Scottish Cup.

But Scot Symon won 15 domestic trophies in 13 years, including two trebles, and took Rangers to two European finals.

He had also been an accomplished player, playing 313 games as one of the club's most loyal men throughout the war.

As boss, he rarely courted the media, giving few interviews, but was an unfailingly honourable man. On the day of the worst result in Rangers' history, the loss to Berwick in 1967 which would have been a bitter pill to the true-blue that Symon was, he sought out the Shielfield Park groundsman and complimented him on what was a very fine playing surface.

James Scot Symon possessed Rangers-type dignity.

■ **Scot Symon (left) with celebrated *Sunday Post* "football man" and Wembley Wizards goalkeeper Jack Harkness.**

■ Mr Symon watching a game at Dens Park, Dundee, when he was still East Fife's manager.

■ A secretive, and somewhat strange, moment in the history of Rangers Football Club management. The first

team squad quietly make their way over Edmiston Drive on their way to The Albion. Turn the page . . .

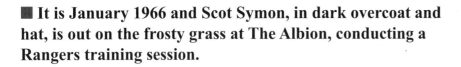

■ **It is January 1966 and Scot Symon, in dark overcoat and hat, is out on the frosty grass at The Albion, conducting a Rangers training session.**

Like Mr Struth before him, Scot Symon had routinely left the handling of these sessions to his trainers, while he dealt with the business of the club.

On this occasion, though, he decided to conduct the training himself – then took the unwise step of banning photographers from attending. This had the effect of greatly exciting the interest of newspaper sports editors. They were agog to know what was going on. So photographers were sent, with telephoto lenses, to find vantage points and glean just what this was all about.

It led to fevered press speculation that Rangers were about to create an internal structure that had a general manager and a head coach – splitting the management duties in two, a European idea that hasn't caught on much in Scotland even now.

■ Scot Symon
with his staff
in 1967.

■ Scot Symon's assistant Bobby Seith. After Mr Symon left, perhaps the role of new manager went to the wrong man. Seith was highly respected within the game, and would go on to be manager of Hearts. He is often cited by players and coaches who worked under him (such as Jim McLean) as having had a huge influence on the way they thought about the game. He was an early advocate of possession-based, Continental-style football.

■ The 1967 Berwick debacle was the death knell for Scot Symon, but it took several months for the hammer to fall. When it did, Davie White was next into the wood-panelled office.

The loyal Seith had resigned in protest at Scot Symon's treatment.

White, however, had also been earning a reputation as an up-and-coming member of the new "tracksuit manager" breed and had steered Clyde to a third-place finish in the First Division of 1966-67, their highest ever placing.

He lasted two years at Ibrox, without winning a trophy, and was the first Rangers manager to be sacked.

Whether he would have been a success as a Rangers manager – if given some more time – is open to debate.

But Rangers don't exist to be runners-up, or beaten finalists in any competition. Rangers managers must be winners.

■ 1969, a properly dignified and genteel Rangers-style welcome for the next manager, the highly-respected former player Willie Waddell.

■ Deedle's first game in the Rangers dug-out was December 13th, 1969 – in torrential rain that turned the Ibrox pitch, and running track, to a glaury mess. Rangers won 2-1 against Dundee United. Much brighter days would follow.

■ **Willie Waddell being introduced to the Press and players on December 8th, 1969.**

Willie had been a star outside-right for Rangers in a war-interrupted career, 1939 to 1955, and knew the standards Mr Struth demanded. But he was also well-versed in the new ideas and demands of modern football. He had been a championship-winning manager of Killie, then a respected journalist.

The day he walked back in the door of the big house was like a breath of fresh air, with a hint of a return of the glory days blowing along beside it.

As with any Rangers manager, Willie divides opinion. He was at times haughty and difficult. But he was also a blue-blooded winner who demanded his team behave and perform in the Rangers way. He steered the club with compassion and dignity in the dark days of the Ibrox disaster, and made himself, and his team, immortal by winning a European trophy.

Willie was also hugely instrumental in creating the modern Ibrox.

Perhaps one of his greatest acts was recruiting Jock Wallace and then moving upstairs when he knew he could leave on-field matters safely in the hands of the younger man.

Willie Waddell was Aye Ready.

■ **Like his predecessor, Jock Wallace was a man of iron will and a habitual winner. Jock never accepted second best.**

All Rangers signings, from now until the end of time, should be sent on a course to learn about what Mr Wallace demanded from his players and what he expected a Rangers player to be.

The photo on the right is from April 29th, 1978. A 2-0 win over Motherwell that confirmed the league championship, on the way to what would be Jock's second treble.

As he would have told you himself: there's not a team like the Glasgow Rangers.

No, not one.

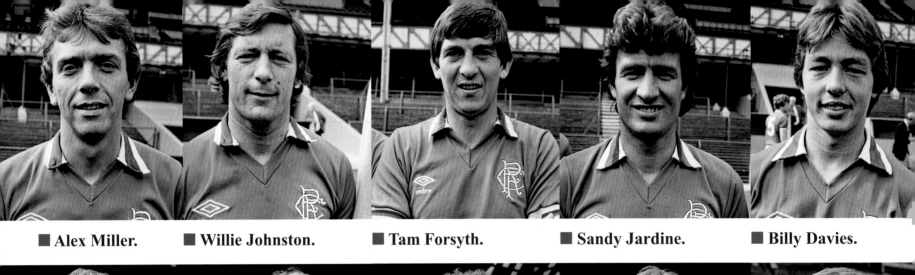

■ Alex Miller. ■ Willie Johnston. ■ Tam Forsyth. ■ Sandy Jardine. ■ Billy Davies.

■ Jim Bett. ■ John McClelland. ■ Peter McCloy. ■ Jim Stewart. ■ Tommy McLean.

■ Davie Cooper. ■ Dave McPherson. ■ Derek Johnstone. ■ Ian Redford. ■ John MacDonald.

■ John Greig deserves a chapter of his own, see page 234.

John took over after Jock Wallace's surprise departure in 1978.

John was a meticulous boss, a tactician, and a football thinker. His team of the early 1980s (left) are sometimes unfairly talked of, but there were some great Rangers men in the line-up.

At this point the club had just spent more than ten times the world record transfer fee on the stadium. No other club had even begun to do this.

The lack of funds for signings due to the reconstruction made the job more difficult for John Greig than for any previous manager.

Just a little of that money to enhance what was, to be fair, an ageing squad might have made John's time in charge a very different part of the club's history.

55

■ John Greig
in 1979, with a model of the
Ibrox project that was about to get under way.

Ibrox

IBROX is a part of Rangers to a larger degree than other clubs are identified with their stadiums.

There could never be a question that Rangers might play at any other venue. No talk of moving to a new ground, no airy-fairy plans for out-of-town developments. Glasgow Rangers play at Ibrox.

The stadium has a majesty, a presence, a character, a history, and most importantly a power that is unique.

It is intimidating to opposing teams, but will also be no small matter to prospective Rangers players. They must be the type of men who can play football at Ibrox. They have to live up to the history, the surroundings, the responsibility of wearing a Rangers shirt, and the magnitude of what it is to run out into that arena.

They have to be able to react to this in the right way. They must have the moral fibre to feel that they belong at Ibrox. And this must come from within them. This is a thing that must be overcome before they can even contemplate playing a game of football.

Once a player is a true Rangers man, however, the history of the place, the rivets in the girders, the foundations, the traditions, give strength on a physical as well as a mental level.

To be a Ranger is a thing you don't rationalise, explain, or even quickly understand. Rangers is a thing you feel. It begins long before you enter Ibrox. You are born with it. Some players are Rangers players before they ever join the club. Some will never be Rangers players despite having played several seasons there. There is no harder place to play football than at Ibrox Park. It takes a special sort of man to be able to do so.

The cornerstone of this truth is worked deep into the structure of Ibrox Park. The stadium has been there beyond the lifespan of any man. The main grandstand says the word "Struth", with all that means.

And every football person who ever stepped inside the old ground – from the most lauded opposition player to the most vehemently denial-ridden supporter of another club – knows it is no small matter to be at Ibrox Park.

It has regularly changed as a stadium, of course. The club has had to evolve, to grow, to improve, to make alterations for safety's sake. The surroundings have had to take on new shapes. This is progress, and Rangers were one of the first clubs in the world to understand the future of football stadiums.

The support might have been sad to see the old coo shed go, and the classic bowl-like shape was, when a good crowd was in, an incredible place to watch a game of football.

But while it had to change, Ibrox is always intrinsically Ibrox.

■ **Right, an aerial view of Ibrox.**

■ **Opposite is Ibrox just before the major renovations to what would become the main "Bill Struth" stand in the mid to late-1920s.**

This was the second Ibrox Park, that Rangers moved to in 1899 after their stay at the first Ibrox (from 1887). The first Ibrox was close by to the east, almost on land that can be seen at the very top of this photo.

The old main stand shown here could hold just under 6,000 on wooden bench-type lines of seats, and was a corrugated iron-clad, steel-framed structure.

The box on top of the stand was for the press, but had become terribly cramped by this point. Many journalists chose to sit in the main part of the stand instead, though there was little enough room there either.

In this photo, the old pavilion had recently been demolished. It stood at the top right corner, as you look.

Almost every ground had a pavilion in the early years of the 20th Century. Purpose-built stands high enough to have offices, dressing rooms and other facilities below the seating area, only began to appear in the 1920s.

Having been built on what was the outskirts of Glasgow at the time, Ibrox was never as badly hemmed in by factories and housing as many British football grounds were, especially in the North of England.

It is also, in comparison to many other grounds, situated on a large site. This gave space and scope for building work to be done, and access to be gained, during redevelopment without closing to supporters or having to relocate many games to other venues.

The first major re-shaping of the ground had much to do with the aftermath of the Ibrox Disaster of 1902, when wooden terracing held up by iron scaffold-like constructions, had collapsed and killed 25 people during a Scotland v. England game.

The Rangers board of the time moved swiftly away from any idea of terraces that weren't concrete or ash, on a slope of firm ground.

The railway line, seen on the left of this photo, was in a deep cutting. It was dug over the course of 1903 (although some work was still going on in 1904) and the earth and rubble was used to build up the banks for the terraces you see here.

However, they continued to grow in a minor way for the next 20 years or so, another step or two being slowly added after earth, stones or rubble had been carried by wheelbarrow to the top of the rim.

The finished result was a bowl of almost uniform height at each end, though dipping towards the railway line side.

The roof on the terrace on the left of the photo (the north) had been relocated from the original Ibrox and had, for many years, a prominent Bovril advert emblazoned on the gable front. It would be replaced in 1954, and would become The Derry, a favourite stance for the Ibrox choir. The back of the old stand also used to carry prominent Bovril adverts.

The capacity of the ground at this time was around 80,000, though that would grow with the huge new stand and its standing enclosure at the front – the new building allowing slightly more pitch-side space than the stand you see here.

IBROX PARK

■ **The main stand at Ibrox, with its imposing entrance, in the 1950s. Left: the mosaic that adorns the main entrance step.**

This is the finest remaining example of an Archibald Leitch construction. In the early 20th Century, Leitch designed the stadiums of Britain's great clubs. Old Trafford, Villa Park, Stamford Bridge, Highbury, Goodison, Hampden, and many more, were his work.

The greatest project for this Glasgow-born, Rangers-supporting giant of architecture, however, was Ibrox. It was his last great undertaking.

The main stand was constructed in two phases. The first was an offices and dressing room block between the existing stand and Edmiston Drive. This was completed in 1927. The second part, 1927-28, and officially opened on January 1st, 1929, was construction of the stand itself. This cost £95,000, the most that had ever been spent on a single grandstand, and a colossal figure at the time.

Red brick is an unusual building material in Glasgow, but then everything about the new Ibrox was new, bigger, and better. It had 10,500 seats, more than any other in the land. The press box was a castellated, eye-catching hilltop fort perched atop the roof.

The X and diagonal-fronted balcony detailing in iron (a trademark feature of Leitch grandstands) has to this day never been covered with advertising – a sign of class and a refusal to compromise that marks Ibrox apart.

Ibrox is the only UK ground where so many Leitch features can still be viewed. Even with the addition of the club deck, there is a keeping of traditions and continuity at The Blue Heaven that is unique.

There is no stadium in the world that retains links with a grand past like Ibrox. It is a football monument.

■ The castellated top of the press box on the main stand in 1961, and (opposite) the renovated version in 1966. The cross and diagonal details on the balcony have been only slightly obscured by the addition of a TV cameras gantry in the 1966 pic.

■ **The Rangers Gates, one of the most iconic football stadium features in the world.**

They are seen here in their original place, at the Copland Road End and were created and installed in 1928, by order of, and to the specification of, Archie Leitch.

They were possibly inspired by the W.G. Grace Gates at Lords cricket ground in London, erected in 1923.

The Ibrox gates are older than any other ornate gates at any British football ground, and have been much copied .

They are the most photographed feature of any football ground in Scotland.

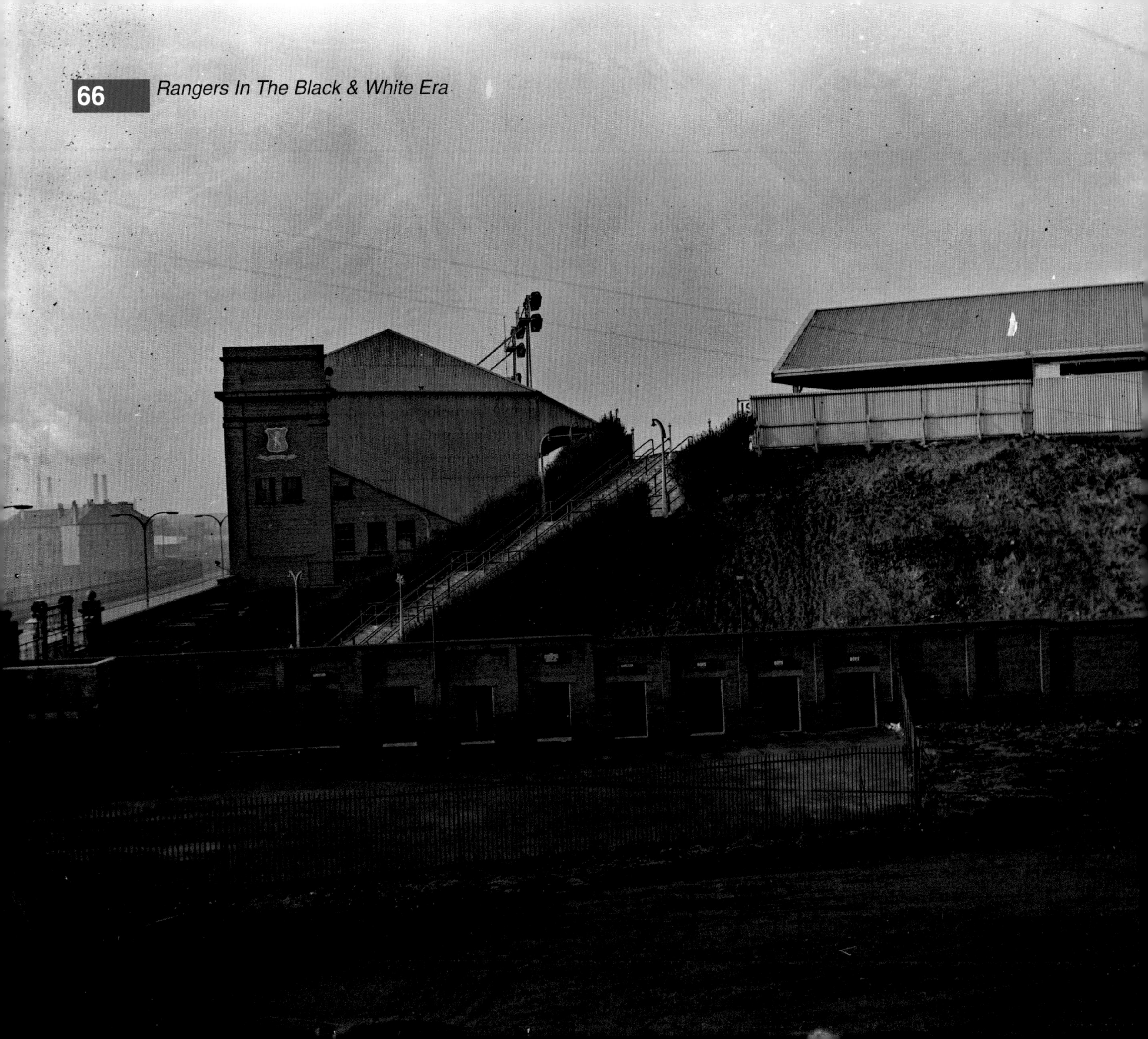

■ Two views of the old stadium from the Copland Road end of Edmiston Drive in the mid-1960s. This is where your father, grandfather, uncles – and probably yourself as a youth – learned what it meant to be a Rangers man.

■ **Scot Symon is presented to the Duke of Edinburgh, who flew in to join The Queen on a Scottish tour, after his helicopter landed on the Ibrox pitch in June 1955.**

Landing a Westland Whirlwind, negotiating it over the Ibrox stand and terracing roofs, would have been quite a sight – and quite a feat of precision piloting. These helicopters had a rotor diameter of 53 feet. A pair of Navy pilots (it took two pilots to handle a Whirlwind), not the duke, did the job.

Even so, Mr Symon would have been wise to have stood well out of the way.

It would be unlikely that such a trick would be attempted in the modern era.

■ **Nothing, not even Ibrox, could stand against Hurricane Low Q, the worst natural disaster to hit Scotland's central belt since records began.**

In the early hours of Monday, January 15th, 1968, the storm produced winds of up to 140 mph, killing 20 people and making more than 700 homeless.

The electricity supply failed in the whole of the Greater Glasgow area, further adding to the terror.

The clean-up operation got under way the next day, and Ibrox was ready for a 40,000 crowd the following Saturday to see Rangers beat Motherwell 2-0.

■ Before Rangers became the first club in Scotland to install undersoil heating in 1981, efforts to keep the playing surface frost-free included a plastic covering, seen in November 1969. It replaced the old system of spreading hay across the pitch.

■ The curves of the terracing behind each of the goals, before the 1970s redesign of Ibrox, were vast. They gave the old bowl-shaped stadium its enormous capacity.

The record crowd is (depending upon the source you take) 118,567 or 118,730, for the 1939 New Year game against Celtic. But both figures are little more than educated guesses. There were many more inside the ground due to lifts over the turnstiles for youngsters, and the other various (and illegal) ways people found to clamber in to the ground.

An estimated further 30,000 were turned away. Of those who did get in, many didn't make it to the top of the stairs, such was the crush, and stood trying to decipher the roars of those who could see the game.

In those days, only international matches (and even then, only those against England) were all-ticket. Football, and Rangers in particular, had grown in popularity so rapidly that few had even thought of safety legislation or regulation of football attendances.

It was quite an experience to be a part of such a crowd. It was noisy, smelly, hemmed-in, and you had to keep your wits about you. The crowd pressed together and swayed or surged with the game's highs and lows. Only the exceptionally tall saw everything that happened on the pitch.

There was no question of going for a Bovril, or visiting the toilet. The passageways were blocked tight with people too. You were there until the game ended and the crowds behind you had dispersed.

Quite apart from the infamous disasters, many injuries happened that were never publicised. Minor crushes against walls, barriers and each other, or ankles being stepped on, were inevitable in what was a seething, sweating, singularity of humanity. It wasn't unusual to lose sight of your friends when a goal was scored, or to find yourself 20 yards away from where you started after the mayhem of the celebrations subsided.

So many gathering in this way wouldn't be permitted in these highly regulated times. It would be viewed as extremely dangerous. But few who remember being in such crowds recall it as anything less than exhilarating. When your team won, and the howls of delight rent the sky, it was as if the joy of those around you multiplied your own excitement.

Nothing even vaguely similar exists these days.

7 EXIT

■ **Right, the Copland Road stand on its introduction to the press in August 1979.**
■ **Above, one of the interior concourses.**
■ **Inset, one of the reasons given for the open corners was that they were a safety feature, allowing easy evacuation from the ground if there was an emergency.**

The disaster of 1971 (see page 82) spelled the end for the old stadium. A new Ibrox was researched, planned and became reality over the turn of the 1970s into the 80s.

There will always be nostalgia for the old ground, but things had to change. What was put in place, all would agree, is an incredible football stadium. The modern-day Ibrox uniquely retains the classic grandeur of Archie Leitch's 1920s design, and melds it with the safety and ease-of-use that modern football demands.

Ibrox has been, for more than 100 years, the most impressive stadium in Britain.

■ Sorry, you'll have had to turn your book on its side to view this properly.

This is Stairway 13. To fully discuss Ibrox, the disaster of 1971 must be mentioned. It gets a chapter to itself in this book.

When it wasn't busy, Stairway 13 wasn't a problem. No worse, certainly, than many other stairs at many other grounds of the time.

What sets it aside is the crowd numbers. In the dark, on frosty concrete, with several thousand people all trying to use it at the same time, it then became a problem. Rangers were, of course, aware of and concerned by this.

But the tragedy happened, and it should not have happened. Ibrox underwent wholesale changes because of it.

■ **Above: Three photos of Rangers Pools winners being presented with their cheques in the 1960s. Furthest left is director Mr David Hope, whose contribution to the development of Rangers, and Ibrox in particular, deserves more recognition.**

Mr Hope started Rangers Pools in 1964 and built it into the most successful organisation of its kind in the football world. Other clubs rushed to copy the model, though few even came close. Millions of pounds were raised over the years, and a lot of lives were changed by the hefty winners' cheques.

The following article and illustration is from 1967 telling how the pools money was to be spent.

The eventual social club looked a little different, but the article outlines a level of forward-thinking that was truly remarkable for its time.

Dedicated club shops? Beaming-back of European ties? Pre-match hospitality for fans? These ideas were unheard of in Scottish football in 1967.

The monetary figures show their age, but at the time were an incredible source of revenue for the club. This money built the Ibrox we know today.

THE SUNDAY POST, DECEMBER 10th, 1967:

RANGERS supporters, to whom Ibrox Stadium is as familiar as their own living-rooms, have a shock coming to them. A pleasant one. Eighteen months from now, they won't recognise the place.

Above (right) is an impression of what the Copland Road end of the stadium will look like by the summer of 1969.

A magnificent new social club will occupy the space at present taken up by a car park and the banking of the east terracing. The final plans were passed last week. Work will

start within the next few months. Total cost of this Ibrox face-lift? £350,000. All part of the Rangers Pools contribution towards making Ibrox the most up-to-date stadium in Europe. The main clubroom will seat over 1000 members.

Looking to the future, the plans provide for the installation of three huge screens. So, when Rangers are taking part in big games on the Continent, closed circuit TV will be showing the game "live" to club members at Ibrox.

Two passenger lifts will operate to all floors. At first-floor level there will be snack bars and coffee lounges to accommodate 300 people – for those wishing a quick snack and a drink before the game rather than a full-scale meal in the main clubroom.

A Rangers "shop" is to be opened in the Reception Hall.

Top-class cabaret stars will provide club members with entertainment in the evenings.

Rangers director Mr David Hope, who is behind the colossal social club enterprise, travelled all over Europe visiting clubs, picked out the best features, and incorporated them all along with his own ideas in the new venture.

The ground will house the new offices for Rangers Pools, which has mushroomed into the biggest money-spinner in British football.

Starting from less than nothing four years ago it looks like passing the 250,000 members mark around New Year. Which will mean a contribution of £2000 a week to Rangers.

If you're the statistically-minded type, you may be interested to know the Pools computer last week revealed that, since the start, the number of shilling contributions paid in now totals 16,999,977.

There's no business like Pools business – if it's handled the right way.

January 2nd, 1971

THERE can be no account given of Rangers in the black and white era without paying respect to those who lost their lives at Ibrox, in the disaster of Saturday, January 2nd, 1971.

There was a crowd of more than 80,000 at the traditional New Year game against Celtic. A few minutes after the final whistle, 66 people died in a crush caused by people falling, then others falling on top of them, at the stairs at the Copland Road end. It was properly called Passageway 13 but known as Stairway 13. A further 200 were injured.

The names of the dead are listed at Ibrox. They are also given here. Rangers will always remember.

Please read them and think of them. Who knows what the 66 would have done, what they would have achieved, what they would have become, in the half century since 1971.

We thought long and hard about which photos to show in this chapter. You may find a few of the images that follow distressing. But they are products of a different time, when newspapers and society were less squeamish about such things. And, after all, this is a book that intends to show what football, and life, was like in another era.

In any case we do not learn, we do not properly pay our respects, if we turn our faces away.

George Adams.
Hugh McGregor Addie.
David Anderson.
Richard Bark.
John Buchanan.
Robert Charles Cairns.
Robert Turner Carrigan.
John Crawford.
Thomas Dickson.
Charles Dougan.
Frankie Dover.
David Cummings Duff.
Peter Gordon Easton.
Peter Gilchrist Farries.
Margaret Oliver Ferguson.
George Crockett Findlay.
Ian Frew.
John Gardiner.
Robert Campbell Grant.
Thomas Grant.
James Graham Gray.
Adam Henderson.
Ian Scott Hunter.
Brian Hutchison.
George McFarlane Irwin.
John Jeffrey.
Andrew Jackson Lindsay.
Charles John Griffiths Livingstone.
James Yuille Mair.
Russell Malcolm.
Robert Maxwell.
Robert McAdam.
Duncan McIsaac McBrearty.

David Douglas McGee.
John James McGovern.
Alexander McIntyre.
John McNeil McLeay.
Richard McLeay.
David Fraser McPherson.
Thomas McRobbie.
Thomas Melville.
Russell Morgan.
Richard Douglas Morrison.
Robert Colquhoun Mulholland.
John Neill.
Alexander Paterson Orr.
David Ronald Paton.
William Mason Philip.
Nigel Patrick Pickup.
James Whyte Rae.
Robert Lockerbie Rae.
Walter Robert Raeburn.
Matthew Reid.
John McInnes Semple.
William Duncan Shaw.
Walter Shields.
James William Sibbald.
George Alexander Smith.
Charles Stirling.
Thomas Walker Stirling.
William Thomson Summerhill.
Donald Robert Sutherland.
Bryan Todd.
James Trainer.
George Wilson.
Peter Wright.

■ The horror unfolded quickly. Each successive minute on the badly-lit stairway revealed an ever-growing number of bodies. Some were laid out on the pitch, others on the indoor running track under the main stand. The Ibrox dressing rooms were turned into makeshift casualty wards.

■ Jock Wallace lent a hand carrying the injured to the waiting fleet of ambulances.

■ Worried relatives gathered at the old Southern & General Hospital, not far from Ibrox, seeking news.

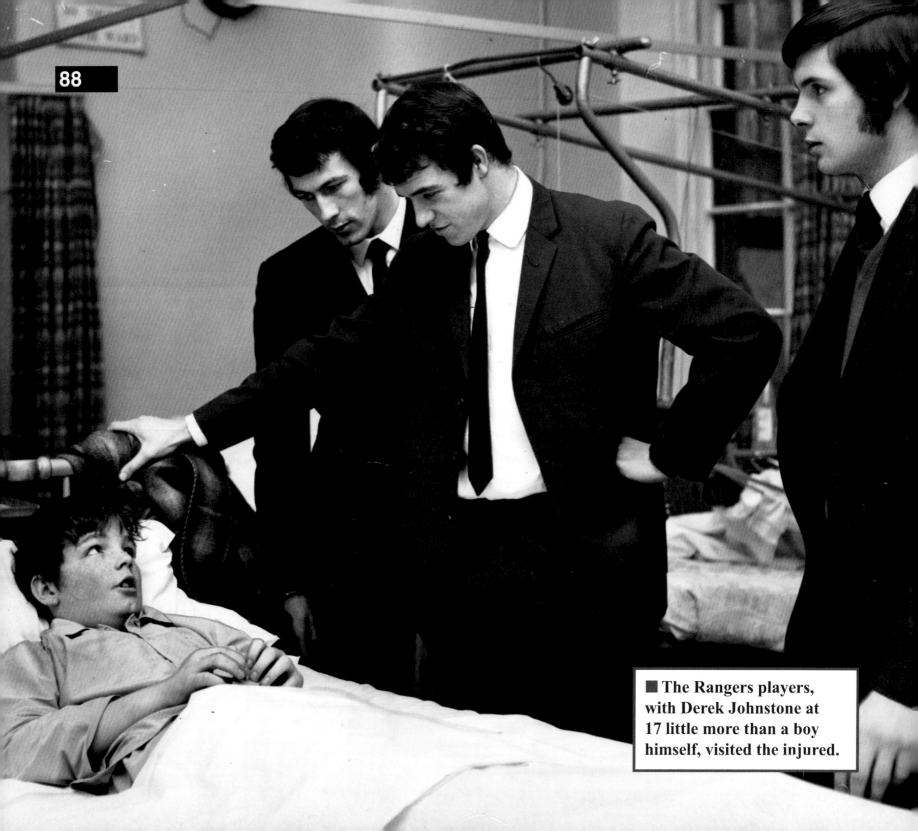

■ The Rangers players, with Derek Johnstone at 17 little more than a boy himself, visited the injured.

■ Rangers manager Willie Waddell, his wife Hilda, and the club directors, at the memorial service at Glasgow Cathedral on January 9th, 1971.

■ **Every funeral told the story of an individual tragedy. Markinch, in Fife, suffered more than most.**

Five young supporters from the village, Peter Easton (13), Bryan Todd (14), Ronald Paton (14), Mason Philip (14), and Douglas Morrison (15) lost their lives.

They had been team-mates, all playing for youth side Markinch United.

This photo shows one of the funeral processions at St Drostan's Church, Markinch.

■ **Right: Many people drew parallels between this tragedy and the 1961 incident on the same stairway that had cost two lives, George Nelson and Thomas Thomson. A further 50 were injured on that occasion.**

■ A two-minute silence was observed before the next game at Ibrox, a 1-1 draw with Dundee United on January 16th, 1971. There was a sombre mood in the drizzle at Ibrox that day for the impeccably-kept respects.

Rangers

. . . Express their deepest sympathy to the relatives of the 66 who lost their lives at Ibrox on January 2, 1971

. . . extend their good wishes for a speedy recovery to the 145 injured

AND

. . . offer their thanks to all those who worked so magnificently under tragic circumstances.

● *Two minutes silence will be observed before today's match.*

■ The programme notes of January 16th, 1971.

■ **During the close season following the disaster a sturdy seven-foot concrete barrier was erected across the top of Stairway 13, and the other Ibrox stairways.**

The plan was to stop fans congregating, waiting for the final whistle before plunging straight down the stairs.

This photo was taken before the Rangers-Tottenham Hotspur friendly on Sunday, August 9th, 1971. The barrier is clear to see at the head of the terracing, although the perspective of this photo doesn't properly capture the height and size of the curved ends of Ibrox.

The game (along with a match against Everton a few days previously) was a dress rehearsal for an 85,000 all-ticket meeting with Celtic scheduled for the following Saturday.

The crowd at the Spurs game was 63,000, and both games against the English clubs passed without incident.

Rangers vowed that a tragedy such as that of January 2nd, 1971, could never happen again. The new Ibrox, shown in the previous chapter, would emerge from these dark days.

Rangers away

WHILE Ibrox, with all its majesty, is home, Rangers – the team and the supporters – are famous throughout the world. The club has always undertaken tours.

The fans also loyally follow Rangers around Scotland, creating home-like crowds at away games.

Season after season, Rangers have filled the stadiums of other clubs. Of the 42 current senior Scottish clubs, 19 of them saw the record attendance at their ground in a game against Rangers.

This is the best-supported club in Scotland, and one of the best-supported in the world. There are hundreds of thousands of Rangers supporters around the globe.

This chapter is by no means a complete record of Rangers away from Ibrox – that would take two or three books to show. It is merely a few examples, a few photos showing the club, the players, and the support when not at Ibrox.

■ **Right: Kilmarnock's Rugby Park on February 12th, 1967, full to bursting-point. The hammer-and-sickle flag was run up to welcome USSR prime minister Alexei Kosygin to the game. Rangers won 2-1.**

1954 Canada and USA tour

CLOSE seasons were longer in the black & white era. In May 1954, Rangers set off for a six-week tour of Canada, which included one game in New York.

This was a highly significant summer for The Rangers. For the first time in 34 years, they were without Mr Struth as manager (see page 26).

The man who would take over, Scot Symon, was still manager of Preston North End at this point, having just seen his men beaten 3-2 by West Bromwich Albion in the FA Cup Final.

Upon leaving for the tour, Sammy Cox had announced that from the following season he would be a full-time footballer, giving up his day job. Perhaps surprising, then, that the following season was to be his last at Ibrox before his transfer to East Fife.

However, the travelling party had injury problems:

WHEN Rangers leave for Canada on Saturday, they'll have six unfit men in their party—Little (back muscle sprain), Caldow and McColl (inoculation reaction), Woodburn (knee twist), Paton (pulled muscle) and Hubbard (foot injury). It's hoped by the time the Empress of Scotland docks at Montreal a week later they'll all be ready to play.

Defender John Little, who had been born in Calgary, Alberta but who grew up in Millport, had agreed to be the *Sunday Post's* correspondent during the tour.

His report from the ground of the Montreal Royals stadium (where he was shocked to learn of the baseball stars' $10,000 salaries) tells: "Like most stadiums in Canada and America, this one is a converted baseball field. Result is there's a raised diamond in one corner and the pitch overlaps on to the ash track. In addition, the boys had to contend with a long-jump pit and a throwing pit inside the touchline, both full of sand."

Undeterred, and in front of an all-ticket crowd, Rangers beat Chelsea in the opening match of the tour.

The Rangers played a total of nine games during the trip. They were:

■ May 16 – (Montreal) Rangers 1, Chelsea 0.

■ May 19 – Rangers 6, Hamilton & District All-Stars 0.

■ May 22 – Rangers 4, Ontario All-Stars 1.

■ May 24 – Rangers 9, British Columbia Mainland All-Stars 0.

■ May 26 – Rangers 7, Victoria 0.

■ May 29 – Rangers 3, Vancouver All-Stars 0

■ June 2 – Rangers 5, Manitoba All-Stars 0.

■ June 5 – (Toronto) Rangers 1, Chelsea 4.

■ June 6 – (New York) Rangers 0, Chelsea 0.

■ Saturday, May 8th, 1954. The Rangers party being piped aboard the Govan-built (of course) *RMS Empress of Scotland* for the cross-Atlantic trip to Montreal.

A crowd of around 200 gathered to give the players what was described as "a rousing send-off."

■ **From left: George Young, Willie Paton, Willie Woodburn, John Prentice, George Niven, Ian McColl, Willie Waddell and Sammy Cox relax (in their Rangers blazers) on the ambitiously-titled "sun deck" of the *RMS Empress of Scotland*.**

It was a choppy crossing.

Rangers reported that "30-foot waves made P.T. impossible on the deck," and "Grierson, Rae, Paton and Caldow all sea sick."

Things changed on arrival, though. John Little made the first of his pre-arranged phone calls to *The Sunday Post* to report: "We had a great reception from hundreds of Scots people when we arrived at the dockside, and the event was shown live on Canadian TV.

"And, boy, is it hot. It's around 80 degrees.

"But we're not complaining. This is the life all right. Most luxurious hotel (It was the 1,000-room Montreal Laurentian) we've ever been in – and that goes for the Chelsea boys too.

"They were already settled in when we arrived. We've now joined forces. Both teams are attending a special dinner tonight."

At the end of the trip, Rangers chairman John Wilson presented all the players with a leather case containing hair brushes as: "a token of the club's appreciation of your conduct and efforts during this memorable tour."

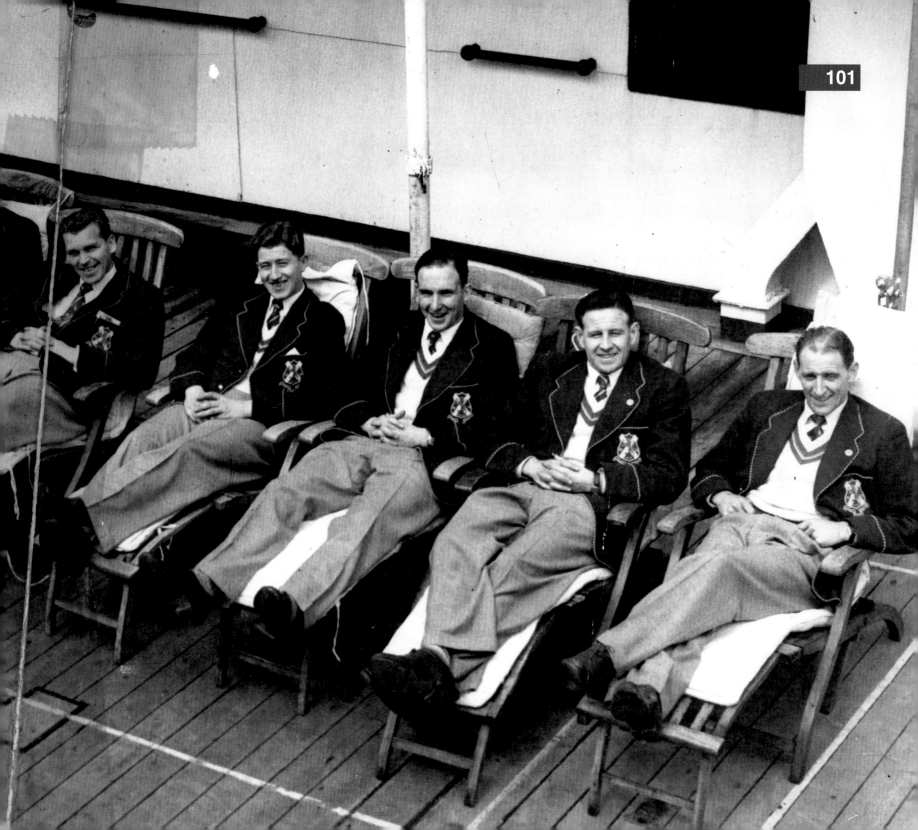

1962 USSR tour

THE summer of 1962 saw Rangers invited on a quite remarkable tour of the USSR.

At the time, the height of the Cold War, Soviet teams didn't take part in European competition as (in their words) "the competitions take place during our off-season". The suspicion in Nato countries, however, was that their players would defect if allowed out of Russia.

However, close season or not, entrance to the European Cup was being considered by the Soviets, and part of the reason for the Rangers trip was so the USSR's best sides could gauge themselves against top-class opposition.

The adventure caught the imagination of football supporters, and politicians, throughout the world. A lot of pressure became attached to these games.

There was an unspoken, but very real, prestige to play for. Nothing that involved competition between East and West was entirely friendly in those days. There was propaganda value in everything, and Scot Symon's team became the representatives of the entire western world.

Rangers won their first game in the Russian capital, 3-1 over Lokomotiv Moscow, then travelled to Georgia to take on Tblisi and beat them too, 1-0. Would the famous Light Blue physical and mental toughness carry them through to beat all the top Soviet sides?

The final game was against Dinamo Kiev in the mighty Khrushchev Stadium. There were rumours that "ringers" from other USSR clubs were being brought in and Rangers would effectively face the national team. Some even said the Russian president himself was to attend in his namesake stadium to spur Kiev on.

There had been no agreement on how many substitutions (not a usual part of football in those days) would be allowed – Rangers only being able to replace a man once the Ukrainians had done so.

And there were a few odd refereeing decisions. For instance, rather than book one of the Kiev players for a scything tackle, the ref marched the Ukrainian offender back to the prone Jimmy Millar and made him give an apologetic speech.

The game was full-blooded, but played mostly in a sporting fashion, and ended in a 1-1 draw. After the final whistle, Rangers were sportingly applauded from the park by the 65,000 fans, with the president of the Ukrainian Football Association saying, "Rangers are easily the best British team we have seen."

Despite the attention paid to the tour by British newspapers, few were prepared for the sight that met The Rangers party when they returned to Renfrew Airport on the evening of Monday, 11th June, 1962. Fully 10,000 fans were there, spilling on to the runway and bringing the airport to a standstill. The west's heroes were home.

■ **Right (and following four pages): Rangers greeted by fans when returning to Renfrew Airport in 1962.**

■ The players were loaded on to a bus for the drive to the terminal building, with Rangers songs belted out all around them.

The crush at the terminal as the players try to get off the bus.

Of course, wherever the team goes in Scotland, the fans follow, follow on. And in the black and white era, this was a longer, dirtier, boozier affair than it is nowadays.

Before Scotland had a proper motorway system any journey on the single-carriageway roads was a major excursion. "Dundee, Hamilton, Aberdeen and back again" took a lot more time.

Every supporter knew the helpless frustration of being stuck in traffic as the clock ticked towards kick-off time.

There were the necessary pit-stops in places like Blackford and Auchterarder, and every bus had its favourite fish and chip shop to visit on the way home.

And there was a lot of drinking involved. Really, an awful lot!

But these were fantastic days out. On buses with no toilets, on trains better suited to cattle than humans, with enough beer to stock an off-licence. Songs were sung, and sometimes composed.

You were with friends, brothers, fathers, and uncles, and there were adventures and misadventures. Sometimes it was a bit rough.

But those days out rank among the most memorable of your life.

■ **The fleets of Rangers buses arriving at Tannadice Park, Dundee, on December 27th, 1975. It was a 0-0 draw.**

■ **Falkirk keeper Dennis Devlin dives at the feet of Willie Johnston.**

■ **The Rangers support filling Brockville to capacity, and beyond, in 1971 – to the point where some supporters have spilled over on to the running track.**

The travelling Rangers support routinely made games like this into a home game. This was good for the team, of course, many times they were roarded on to victory.

Football economics were different in those days. Until 1980, clubs split the gate money for all league games.

The game shown here, Falkirk v. Rangers on September 18th, 1971, drew a crowd of 24,000 – greatly above The Bairns' average attendance, though Rangers took half of the receipts.

But take, for instance, the Rangers v. Hibs game at Ibrox on April 29th, 1950. It was a titanic clash, both clubs vying for the title. The crowd that day was 101,000. Hibs took the receipts from 50,500 of those Ibrox customers, but certainly didn't bring 50k supporters with them.

Slim Jim Baxter. Natural.

WITHOUT any further qualifying comment, without having to reference any other player, without resorting to the phrase "among the", Jim Baxter was the best footballer Scotland has ever produced.

Slim Jim is probably best remembered for his gallus keepie-ups at Wembley in the win of 1967, but in reality his best years were 1960 to 1964 at Ibrox – before his leg break – when, week in, week out, he was unplayable. No one could get near him. He did exactly what he wanted to do with the ball. He could fire a raking, defence-splitting pass, or shift himself into third gear (rarely higher) and ghost past all and any player facing him.

If some fast runner caught up, Jim just chopped back, changed direction, and left them skidding in his wake.

He was extremely difficult to tackle. Defenders wait for a small flaw, a push of the ball just an inch too far, a slight shiver in balance, before they pounce. Baxter rarely gave such chances.

One of the best ways to judge a player is to look at the on-field situation when he gets the ball, then the situation when he parts with the ball. When Jim parted with the ball, defence had turned to attack or midfield play had become a chance of a goal.

It is an enormous loss to world football that more footage hasn't survived, or was never recorded in the first place, of Baxter's natural, easy, heaven-sent talent.

There is some film of him, however, and it should be studied. Baxter's loping stride, with the ball always under control, is unlike almost any other footballer's style of play before or since. At times he looks like he is walking. Moving with the ball, he pushes it precisely far enough in front for it to be waiting in his stride pattern for his next touch – usually with that left foot.

He never looks ruffled, never even looks like he is trying very hard. His talent is such that everything seems natural. He doesn't have to think about ball control, it comes under his spell as if it wants to be controlled.

And he could do everything. He wasn't a dribbler, a speed merchant, a tackler, a shooter, a dead-ball expert, or a distributor. He was all of those things.

There has never been a player in Scotland, and very few others around the world, who was so relaxed and so comfortable on a pitch with a ball at his feet.

It must be remembered that he mostly did all this on surfaces that were sometimes rutted, puddle-strewn mud-piles. But there is no mystery in it, no hyperbolic claims that he did it "by magic". The explanation is simple. Jim could control a ball bobbling over divots, a ball stuck in the mud, or a ball skidding on frost – because his timing and eye-to-foot co-ordination allowed him to control anything.

And, to his eternal credit and in stark contrast to an awful lot of footballers, Jim had a sense of humour that shone through on the park and off it.

■ Jim and pals during his National Service with The Black Watch.

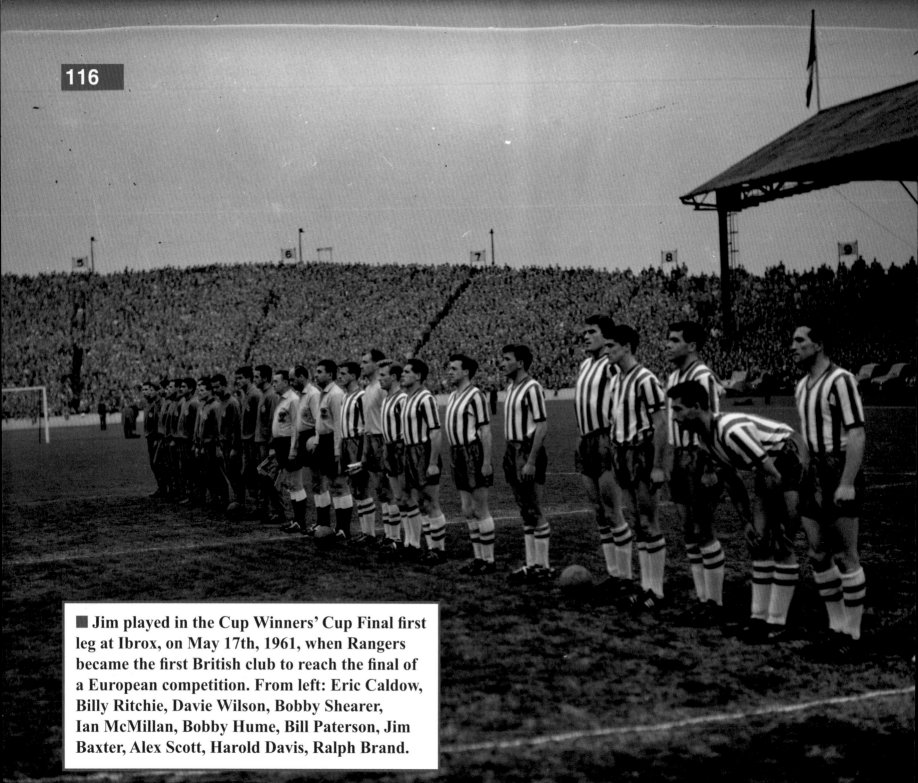

■ Jim played in the Cup Winners' Cup Final first leg at Ibrox, on May 17th, 1961, when Rangers became the first British club to reach the final of a European competition. From left: Eric Caldow, Billy Ritchie, Davie Wilson, Bobby Shearer, Ian McMillan, Bobby Hume, Bill Paterson, Jim Baxter, Alex Scott, Harold Davis, Ralph Brand.

■ Scot Symon made him captain in 1964, thinking it might give an added sense of responsibility. If nothing else, Jim found it amusing.

■ Slim Jim was a superstar of his time, a cult hero, an early example of the celebrity-footballer-personality figure that exists in a more bloated manner today.

The magnitude of the interest in his first wedding, to Jean Paterson, in June 1965, took most people by surprise.

The crowd that gathered outside Garturk Parish Church, Whifflet, was unprecedented for Scotland, never mind a wee place beside Coatbridge.

This was a new thing for a nation where the people were renowned for being canny, reserved, and unimpressed by anyone they thought might be getting above themselves.

This was a sprinkling of stardust. A handsome, talented hero and his stunningly beautiful, fashion model-like bride.

Training

RANGERS were always the fittest team in the Scottish league in the black and white era. There was never a compromise on that, never any question that it should be so.

There were no shortcuts to this status, however. There was only one way to make sure of it. Hard, hard work.

These photos show Rangers doing that training.

There is the famous (or infamous, if you ever had to do it) murder hill at Gullane Sands, of course, but there was much more to Rangers training than that.

On many occasion, training took place at The Albion Greyhound Track, not far from Ibrox. It saw use as a racing venue from 1928 to 1959, when Rangers took it on as their training ground. But it also provided car parking for members and media on match days.

It was in use as a training venue until the mid-1980s, when Graham Souness decided that the team required better facilities and had them training elsewhere (generally at rugby grounds around Glasgow) until Murray Park was built.

The Albion is still a match day car park, though there have been moves to use part of the land for housing.

In the background of some of The Albion photos you'll see the Broomloan Court high-rise flats, which were demolished in 2010.

■ **Left: Jock Wallace at The Albion in 1973.**

■ October 1970. John Greig leads the way up murder hill.

■ **The way it used to be.**

Rangers have always paid a lot of attention to, and invested money in, their training system. It is a club tradition.

The recruitment of Mr Struth in 1914 was largely because his athletics-style player conditioning had been paying dividends at Clyde.

At the distance of a century, these 1920s shots look primitive. But this was the cutting edge of physical preparation at the time, an approach that included exercising all of the muscles of the body, not just the legs. It was the envy of Scottish football.

And it worked. Rangers dominated the league championship in the 1920s.

■ **Left: Dougie Gray leapfrogs Dr James Marshall.**

■ **Right: Tommy Muirhead, Billy McCandless, Jimmy Simpson, John Buchanan, and Bob McGowan lap the Ibrox track. Note the substantial rope-climbing apparatus, that must have been an exercise in itself to carry, in the background.**

Gullane

GULLANE SANDS was more than just a training venue for Jock Wallace's Rangers, it was a psychological weapon.

The workouts, sprints up the dunes of the East Lothian town's beach, facing the Forth estuary, were punishing. The players called it "murder hill" and they were made to run up it, every footstep falling away a few feet into the soft sand, carrying weights or even fellow players.

Some called it brutal, some called it inhumane, most didn't have the breath to call it anything at all. It wasn't unusual for players to vomit with exhaustion – which Jock saw as a sign of a player working properly.

But once the news was out, and it became widely reported in the papers, that The Rangers did this, it added to the super-fit supermen aura Jock's teams had.

They were the best. They could do what other teams could not. Even Rangers players believed this to be true.

You've got to admire the power of one simple training routine that instills a sense of fear into the opposition and a feeling of self-belief into your own players.

No fool, Mr Wallace.

■ **When it came to training, Roger Hynd was in a league of his own.**

He was an international-class athlete, as can be seen from his gymnastic prowess. The nephew of Liverpool guru Bill Shankly, he didn't have a long Rangers career but fits well into the club's tradition of imposing centre-halfs. After leaving Ibrox in 1969 he had a lengthy career south of the Border, most notably with Birmingham City, and was briefly Motherwell manager before becoming, unsurprisingly, a PE teacher.

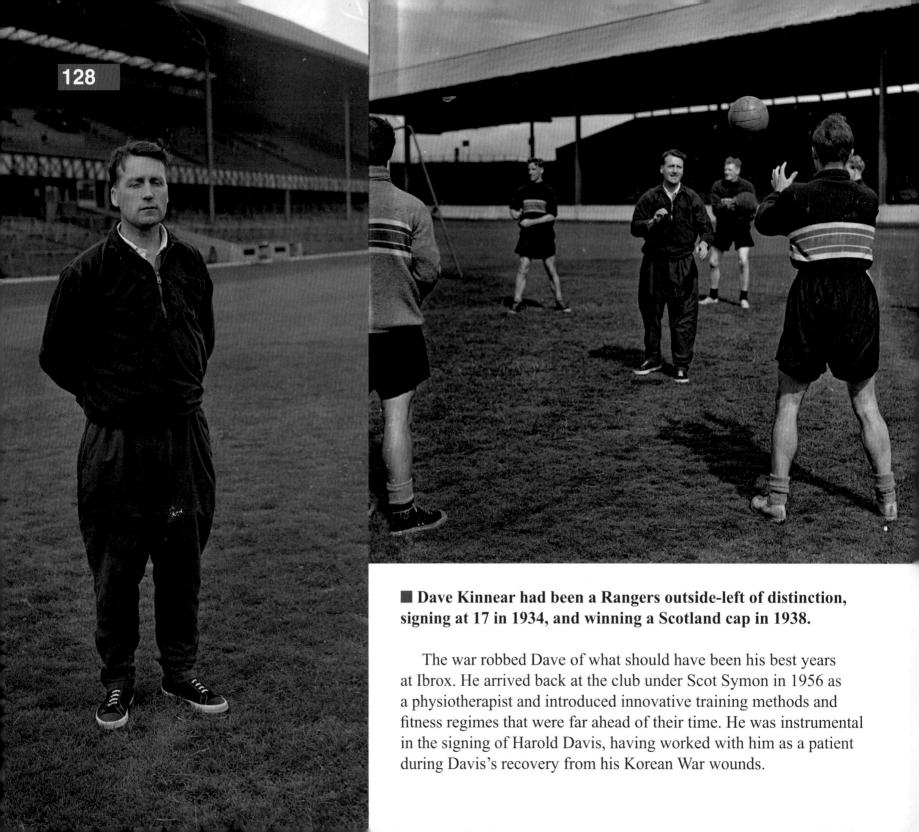

■ **Dave Kinnear had been a Rangers outside-left of distinction, signing at 17 in 1934, and winning a Scotland cap in 1938.**

The war robbed Dave of what should have been his best years at Ibrox. He arrived back at the club under Scot Symon in 1956 as a physiotherapist and introduced innovative training methods and fitness regimes that were far ahead of their time. He was instrumental in the signing of Harold Davis, having worked with him as a patient during Davis's recovery from his Korean War wounds.

■ **Above and left: Willie Henderson working out with legendary trainer Joe Aitchison at Dalmarnock Amateur Boxing Club in August 1965. Joe was highly respected in the fight game, being involved in the careers of many of the greats of Scottish boxing.**

Willie wasn't a tall laddie. So to survive the often brutal tackling – which was regarded as fair play in the 1960s, a part of the game – he had to be robust. He had to be fit enough to handle the hard knocks. These photos show that he took this training seriously. He looks lean, well-muscled – a proper boxer.

RACE
RUNNERS 1 2 3 4 5
TIME

■ The Rangers
first-team squad
stretching at
The Albion.

■ **The Albion in 1958.** To the right is Moore Park, home of St Anthony's Juniors, who played in green-and-white hoops. Further up is the original Tinto Park, home of Benburb, who played in Rangers colours. Bens v. Ants encounters were always keenly-contested.

◄ **Tinto Park.**

■ **Moore Park.**

■ **The Albion.**

■ **Ibrox.**

■ Slim Jim vaults his way on to The Albion pitch.

THE three men on the right are wearing the 1920s Rangers training kit – wool polo-necked jersey tucked in to cotton shorts.

Trainingwear at most clubs was left-over shirts, or simmets the players brought in themselves. But Rangers, thanks to Mr Struth's love of conformity and insistence on the best of everything for his players, provided a training uniform. The new main stand housed a laundry

This was an era of intervention on strips by the authorities, in a bid to impose uniformity across the game. For season 1927-28, the Scottish Football League decreed all clubs must wear white shorts when playing at home, black for away. But this rule was widely flaunted and didn't last long.

Conversely, yellow jerseys became mandatory for goalkeepers in internationals from 1921, which was widely adhered to for decades even in club matches.

Numbers on strips didn't become compulsory in Scotland until 1960, though Rangers had been wearing numbered shirts for many years.

The first Rangers short-sleeved shirts also appeared in 1960, at the same time as the V-necked "Continental style" of a tighter-

■ **From left: Bob McDonald (Rangers 1928-38), Bobby Ireland (1922-30), and Tom Lockie (1927-31).**

fitting shirt, replacing the baggy, button-necked long-sleeved jerseys that had been worn since before the war, and would be worn for several further decades by rugby teams.

In 1968 the famous round-necked shirt, Rangers blue with blue collar, replaced the V-necks and would stay for a decade. It remains the iconic

look for the generation of fans who grew up in that era.

But training shirts of that time (as modelled in 1969 by Jim Baxter and Alex Ferguson on the facing page) were still thick cotton, sometimes quilted, and often deemed too hot . . . which clearly sparked discussions about the weather!

■ Derek Johnstone jumps wooden hurdles (which took scrapes out of shins if misjudged) at The Albion in 1979, with Ibrox in the background behind the buildings on Hinshelwood Drive.

■ 1973. Jock Wallace gives orders during pre-season sprints. This must have been a particularly tough session, as even Sandy Jardine looks out of breath. Note that all the players are still in identical kits, even down to the Adidas Sambas. And every man has his socks pulled all the way up. This is, after all, The Rangers.

Rangers line-ups

R ANGERS did pre-season team line-up photos better than any other club, and with a purpose that didn't exist at any other club. They look like Guards regiments.

The players in the line-up photos could be mistaken for Greek gods. They all sported (as Mr Struth would have insisted) good haircuts, clean-shaven faces, well-laundered strips, with each man in identical arms-crossed pose. They looked like what they were – a unit of formidable athletes.

To achieve this once or twice, would be one thing, but Rangers line-ups looked the same decade after decade. The faces changed, but the photo composition was consistent.

There was a psychological message in this. The intention was to show that Rangers were the best. Mr Struth would have his men march, bowler-hatted and dressed in suits and greatcoats, into opposition stadiums for away games. They looked like a different breed, a caste of gentlemen warriors. The same thing is shown in the team photos, and this idea stayed in place long after Mr Struth retired in 1954.

A Rangers line-up photograph is a display of power.

This isn't a complete set of photos year by year. It is, however, probably the most Rangers team photos ever assembled in one place.

And some are damaged. I could have had them digitally mended, but there is authenticity in the photos as they are. They are fragile, sometimes tattered, artefacts. But handling these 100-year-old documents is like touching history.

I have tried to recreate that here.

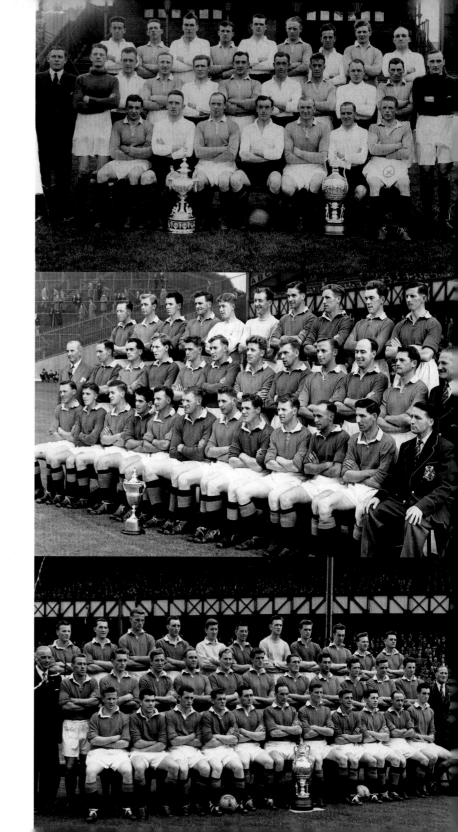

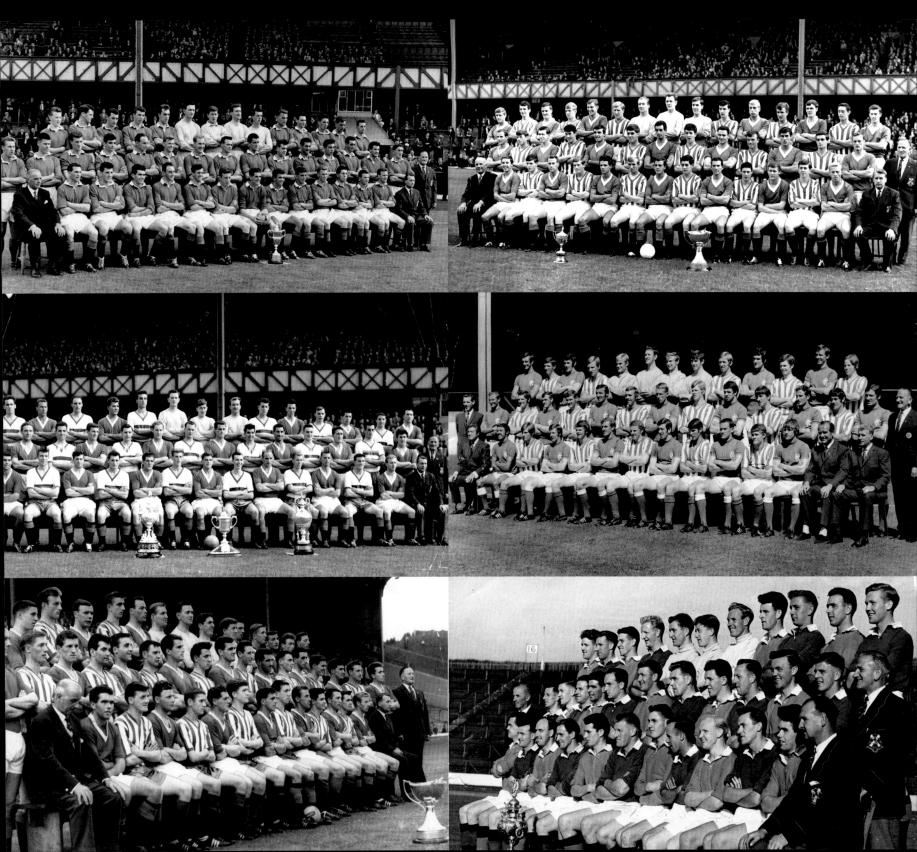

1920

■ **Rangers Football Club, 1920-21.**

The revered William Wilton had just died in what has often been called "a boating accident", though he was lost while trying to climb from a yacht, on to the quayside, in a severe storm. In any case, Mr William Struth, at the request of the board (and after some hesitation on his part) took on the job.

This was a significant point in the story of The Rangers.

Mr Struth isn't in this photo, team training matters being overseen by George Livingstone. But he probably oversaw matters from behind the camera and his influence on the club would become ever more apparent. Already we see the regimented approach to line-ups. This team would be champions that year.

There are players who were signed to the club but are missing from this photo, and the inset men's names aren't in the caption. Although at the distance of a century it is difficult to know why.

Back, from left: James Smith, George McQueen, Davie Meiklejohn, Hector Lawson, James Sutherland, Thomas McDonald, Robert McMillan.

Middle: George Livingstone (trainer), James Walls, Tom Reid, Herbert Lock, Robert Manderson, Willie Robb, Harold McKenna, Sandy Archibald.

Front: Alex Laird, Arthur Dixon, Geordie Henderson, James Bowie, John Law, Tommy Muirhead, Alex Johnston, Alan Morton.

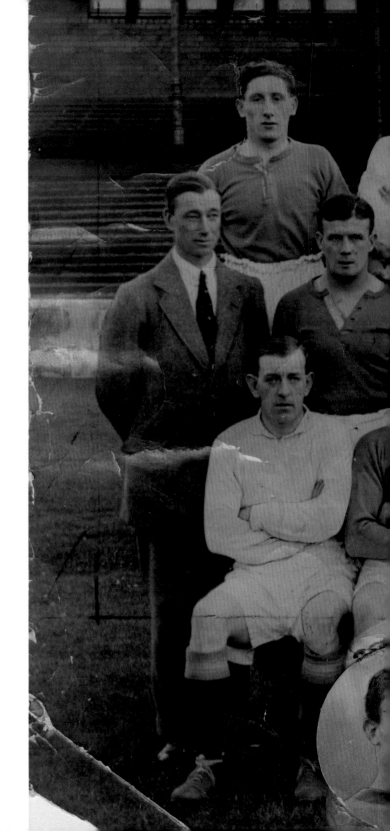

1921

■ **Rangers Football Club 1921-22.**

The club were already a huge force in Scottish football by the time the 1920s dawned. But, under the management of Mr Struth, The Rangers were about to cement their place not only as the pre-eminent Scottish club, but one of the greatest footballing institutions in the world.

Mr Struth still doesn't appear in this (sadly damaged) photo that was taken in front of the ornate old pavilion which stood at the south-east corner of Ibrox, but was soon to be swept away with the remodelling of the ground in the mid-1920s.

Back row, from left: Robert McDermid, Tom Reid, Frank Roberts, James Morton, Hector Lawson, Andy Kirkwood, William Fowler, Alex Johnston, James Low.

Middle: George Livingstone (trainer), Willie Robb, Sandy Archibald, Robert Manderson, James Bowie, Harold McKenna, James Walls, James Smith, William Gould.

Front: Billy McCandless, Tommy Cairns, T. Marshall, Andy Cunningham (captain), Arthur Dixon, Geordie Henderson, Davie Meiklejohn, Alan Morton.

1923

■ **Rangers Football Club 1923-24.**

This team were runaway League champions and Glasgow Cup winners. These were the years of the sustained dominance Rangers exerted between the wars. Mr Struth appears in a team photo for the first time and was by this point fully exerting his personality upon the club. He stands beside Tom Hamilton, one of The Rangers' greatest goalkeepers, who he had recently signed from Kirkintilloch Rob Roy.

This was the season that Carl Hansen would break his leg. He never played for The Rangers again, but is fondly remembered. Rangers had toured Denmark in 1921 and been impressed not only by Hansen's attacking prowess, but his dignified demeanour. He conducted himself like a Rangers man. So, paying his club, Boldklubben 1903, a fee of £20, the "Great Little Dane" was eventually persuaded to become his country's first professional footballer and the first foreign national to score in an Old Firm match (see also page 283).

Back, from left: Murdoch McDonald, Willie Reid, Andy Kirkwood, James Walls, James Kilpatrick, Bobby Ireland, Willie Robb, Frank Roberts, Billy McCandless.
Middle: Mr Struth (manager), Tom Hamilton, Davie Meiklejohn, John Jamieson, Tully Craig, John Nicholson, Geordie Henderson, Alex Johnston, Arthur Dixon, Hector Lawson, Willie Robb, George Livingstone (trainer).
Front: Sandy Archibald, Tommy Muirhead, Tommy Cairns, Robert Manderson, Andy Cunningham, Alan Morton, Carl Hansen.

1928

■ Rangers Football Club 1928.

This is an early, and again damaged, example of what would eventually become known as a "newspaper graphic". The intention is to show the team in its 2-3-5 formation – and this was one of the most famous Rangers teams of all time.

This was the line-up that beat Celtic 4-0 to win the Scottish Cup for the first time in quarter of a century, and comfortably take the league, to record the club's first ever "double".

Many more would follow.

These men deserve the fullest respect – 11 winners, urged on to great heights by Mr Struth. This was quite a team. The centenary of their feat, when it comes, deserves to be greatly celebrated by the club.

Top: goalkeeper Tom Hamilton.
Back, from left: right-back Dougie Gray and left-back Robert Hamilton.
Middle: right-half Jock Buchanan, centre-half Davie Meiklejohn, and left-half Tully Craig.
Front: outside-right Sandy Archibald, inside-right Andy Cunningham, centre-forward Jimmy Fleming, inside-left Bob McPhail, and outside-left Alan Morton.

1929

■ **Rangers Football Club 1929-30.**

The famous "Grand Slam" team.

Rangers won every competition they entered in 1929-30, an unprecedented achievement.

They won the League, Scottish Cup, Glasgow Cup and Glasgow Merchants' Charity Cup. The Charity Cup, as per the rules, was won on a coin toss after a 2-2 draw in the final. The reserves won the Alliance League and Second XI Cup.

Rangers then took a 16-player party on an extensive tour of North America, winning all 14 games they played and scoring 68 goals. The send-off at Greenock came immediately after the Charity Cup Final and the dockside was thronged with thousands of Rangers men, singing *Follow Follow* to see the team off.

This was one of the all-time-great Rangers teams.

Back, from left: James Kerr (trainer), Davie Meiklejohn, James Marshall, Sandy Archibald, Jimmy Fleming, Tom Hamilton, Jock Buchanan, Tom Craig, Mr Struth (manager).
Front: George Brown, Dougie Gray, Bob McDonald, Tommy Muirhead (captain), Bob McPhail, Robert Hamilton, Willie Nicholson, Alan Morton.

1931

■ **Rangers Football Club, 1931-32.**

This Rangers side was to win the Scottish Cup, and this was the season that Northern Irishman Sam English, a fast and highly skilled striker, set the club's goalscoring record, with 44 goals in 35 league games. When Scottish and local cups goals are taken into account, English's tally was 56.

Rangers had been going for a sixth successive league title, but were runners-up to the best ever side in Motherwell's history.

This season also saw the tragedy of goalkeeper John Thomson's death in the Old Firm encounter of September 5th, 1931, after a collision with English. Mostly due to ill-informed barracking because of the accident, Sam English would move from Rangers within two years.

Back, from left: Tom Hamilton, Jimmy Fleming, Jock Buchanan, Sam English, Matthew Hailstones, George Brown, Bobby Main, Robert McAulay, Jerry Dawson,
Middle: Mr Struth (manager), Robert Hamilton, James Marshall, Jimmy Smith, Bob McPhail, William Deans, Sandy Archibald, Jimmy Simpson, William Nicholson,
Front: George Conlin, Bob McDonald, John Murray, Davie Meiklejohn, Robert McGowan, Dougie Gray, Tully Craig, Alan Morton, James Kerr (trainer).

1933

■ **Rangers Football Club 1933-34**

The 1920s and '30s were a time of extraordinary Ibrox dominance. In the two decades before the Second World War, The Rangers won 15 Scottish championships.

This 1933 team, however, had a unique distinction. The Arsenal won five English championships in the 1930s, including three in a row, 1933, '34 and '35. There was a long tradition of Woolwich Arsenal v. Rangers meetings, stretching back to Victorian times, the two clubs being the greatest institutions in football. To decide the best team in Britain, Rangers played Herbert Chapman's "Bank of England" Gunners over two legs, on September 20th and 27th, 1933, beating them home and away, 2-0 at Ibrox and 3-1 at Highbury, in front of huge crowds. Rangers were world champions.

This is a brittle and badly damaged photo, a piece of Rangers history. It is mounted on a cardboard backing, which is unusual for the time – although the cardboard is now in a bad state of repair.

Back, from left: Jerry Dawson, Jimmy Simpson, John Drysdale, Jimmy Smith, Charles Mason, James Kennedy, William Deans, John Russell, Tom Hamilton.

Middle: Mr Struth (manager), Bob McPhail, Tom Russell, Sandy Archibald, William Cheyne, Robert McAulay, James Wilson, Tully Craig, Hugh Boyd, Willie Nicholson, Arthur Dixon (trainer).

Front: Bobby Main, Thomas Hart, Alec Stevenson, Dougie Gray, Torry Gillick, Davie Meiklejohn, Jimmy Fleming, Bob McDonald, James Marshall, George Brown.

1935

■ **Rangers Football Club 1935-36.**

The team who would win a third Scottish Cup in succession, the first time this had been done in the 20th Century.

Such was the popularity of The Rangers at this point, and such were the crowds, that plans were drawn up to redevelop Ibrox to give a 200,000 capacity.

This season was also the last played by the archetypal Rangers captain David Ditchburn Meiklejohn, a model for all captains of the club to follow, and one of the greatest Rangers of all time (see also page 290).

Back, from left: Jerry Dawson, William Cheyne, Thomas Hart, Thomas Brownlie, Thomas McKillop, Bobby Main, George Jenkins.
Middle: Mr Struth (manager), Bob McDonald, Walter Hay, Jimmy Simpson, James Kennedy, Jimmy Smith, John Drysdale, Bob McPhail, John McHarg, Frank Roberts, Arthur Dixon (trainer).
Front: Alec Venters, Alex Winning, George Brown, Robert McAulay, Davie Meiklejohn, Davie Kinnear, Torry Gillick, James Fiddes, Dougie Gray.

1948

■ Rangers Football Club 1948

It wasn't "The Treble" in those days, it was "The Triple Crown".
It had never been done before, although this was because the
League Cup hadn't existed. It must be said that several of the great
Rangers teams of the pre-war era would have been well equipped to
lift three national trophies in a season.

Rangers had re-started after the war in the same powerful way
that they had left off. If any team in Scotland wanted to win a
trophy, they had The Rangers to reckon with.

This was the renowned Rangers team of the "Iron Curtain"
defence (see page 8), with some men displaying the blue and white
hooped away shirts of that time.

**Back, from left: George Scobie, Willie Waddell, David
Marshall, Bobby Brown, Dennis Wright, George Niven, John
McPherson, Eddie Rutherford, James Letters, Adam Little.**

**Middle: Mr Struth (director-manager), Duncan Stanners,
George Young, Archie McIndewar, Ian McColl, Jimmy Parlane,
Willie Woodburn, Jimmy Frame, Willie Findlay, Rex Dunlop,
Willie Rae, Donald McDonald, Billy Williamson, Jimmy Caskie,
Jimmy Smith (trainer).**

**Front: John McIntyre, Willie Thornton, John Lindsay,
Torry Gillick, Willie Paton, Jock Shaw (captain), Billy Arnison,
Sammy Cox, Joe Johnson, Jimmy Duncanson, Tom McAdam.**

1954

■ **Rangers Football Club 1954-55.**

The first season of Scot Symon.

Mr Struth – the greatest football manager of all time – was, of course, a hard act to follow. This was made even more difficult for his replacement Symon by the fact that the former manager, when his health would allow, was often to be seen in and around Ibrox.

Scot Symon was, however, a strong personality, and very much his own man. He did things his way and made swingeing changes to the staff. Fully a dozen of the players in this line-up do not appear when you turn the page to the 1955 pre-season photo.

Back, from left: Andrew Simpson, Jim Rodger, William McRae, Gordon McKenzie, Willie Woodburn, George Niven, John Neil, Bobby Brown, Bobby Carmichael, Colin Liddell, Ross Menzies, John Woods, Ian Neillands.

Middle: Scot Symon (manager), William Simpson, Alan Elliot, Willie Waddell, Jim Pryde, Ian McColl, Duncan Stanners, John Prentice, William McCulloch, William Paton, Eric Caldow, Johnny Hubbard, Joe Craven (assistant trainer).

Front: Hamish McMillan, Derek Grierson, Hunter MacMillan, Sammy Cox, Don McIntosh, George Young, George McKenzie, John Little, William Gardiner, William Findlay, Ralph Brand, Jim Smith (trainer).

The trophy is the Glasgow Cup.

1955

■ **Rangers Football Club, 1955-56.**

This team would be champions of the newly-renamed First Division (it had been known as the A Division since the war).

But they exited the Scottish Cup at the quarter-final stage, to eventual winners Hearts, and lost in the semi-final of the League Cup to eventual winners Aberdeen.

At this point, this was regarded as not one of the better Rangers seasons.

Back, from left: Jimmy Walker, Billy Simpson, Willie Boyd, Willie Gardiner, Billy Ritchie, George Niven, Bobby Brown, Harry Lawrie, Adam Menzies, Ian Neillands, Johnny Woods,

Middle: Scot Symon (manager), John Little, Allan Elliot, Willie Waddell, Jim Pryde, Ian McColl, Duncan Stanners, John Prentice, Max Murray, Willie Paton, Sandy Thomson, Eric Caldow, Joe Craven (assistant trainer);

Front: Willie McCulloch, Derek Grierson, Willie Rae, Sammy Cox, John Queen, George Young, Billy Smith, Johnny Hubbard, Bobby Cunning, Hunter McMillan, Alex Scott, Jimmy Smith (trainer);

1956

■ **Rangers Football Club 1956-57.**

This was the first Rangers team to take part in European competition, and which also retained the Scottish championship. The Rangers exited the European Cup at the hands of French title-winners OGC Nice, after an aggregate 3-3 draw – 2-1 (at Ibrox) and 1-2 (in Nice) – forced a play-off at the not entirely neutral venue of the Parc des Princes in Paris.

The 65,000 crowd that attended the Ibrox leg of the Nice tie, on October 24th, demonstrated the Rangers public's appetite for this novel idea of international club football, and so changed the outlook of the club for ever after.

Winning league championships is Rangers' business, and always will be. But for ever after that October evening in 1956 there was the European stage to consider.

The European competitions were created with the purpose of allowing the continent's great sides to measure themselves against one another. To function as it was designed to do, European football needs clubs of the stature of Rangers.

Back, from left: Willie Paton, Ross Menzies, Max Murray, Billy Arnison, George Niven, Billy Ritchie, Willie Logie, Billy Simpson, Alan Austin, John Little.
Middle: Scot Symon (manager), Ian McColl, Willie McCulloch, Sammy Baird, Willie Moles, Don Kitchenbrand, Jimmy Walker, John Prentice, John Atkinson, Willie Rae, Stewart McCorquodale, Joe Craven (assistant trainer).
Front: Sandy Thomson, Eric Caldow, Allan Elliot, Alex Scott, Derek Grierson, George Young, Billy Smith, Bobby Shearer, Davie Wilson, Johnny Hubbard, Jim Dodds, Davie Kinnear (trainer).

1957

■ **Rangers Football Club, 1957.**

This wouldn't be a great season for The Rangers. The team photo is significant for what is not in it – the inspirational figure of George Young, who had retired.

Good team or bad team, however, this is an excellent example of the Rangers pre-season line-up photo. It has an air of majesty. This photo, packed with clean-cut, wholesome young men with something of a military bearing, is clearly a demonstration of power.

There's not a club like the Glasgow Rangers.

Back, from left: Billy Smith, Jimmy Millar, John Atkinson, Willie Logie, Charlie Wright, George Niven, Billy Ritchie, John Valentine, Hugh Neill, Harold Davis, Alan Austin.

Middle: Max Murray, John Currie, Billy Simpson, Willie Stevenson, Robert Morrison, Jimmy Walker, Sammy Baird, Willie Moles, Don Kitchenbrand, Sandy Thomson, John Little, John Queen, Joe Craven (assistant trainer).

Front: Scot Symon (manager), Eric Caldow, George Duncan, Alex Scott, Tom Robertson, Ian McColl (captain), Stewart McCorquodale, Johnny Hubbard, Ralph Brand, Bobby Shearer, Harry Melrose, Davie Wilson, Davie Kinnear (trainer).

1958

■ **Rangers Football Club 1958.**

This team would return the league championship to Ibrox, its rightful home, although only after a very tight finish to the season.

A few names appear for the first time, men who would be important in the years to come. Another great Rangers team was being built.

Back, from left: Brian McIlroy, Ralph Brand, Bobby Orr, John Currie, George Niven, John Little, Norrie Martin, Willie Moles, Alan Austin, Davie Wilson, Stewart McCorquodale.

Middle: Scot Symon (manager), Jimmy Millar, Billy Smith, Billy Simpson, John Valentine, Sammy Baird, Bill Paterson, Willie Telfer, Harold Davis, Billy Hogg, Hugh Neill, Max Murray, Joe Craven (assistant trainer).

Front: George Duncan, Alex Scott, John Queen, Bobby Shearer, Andy McEwan, Ian McColl, Willie Stevenson, Eric Caldow, Andy Matthew, Johnny Hubbard, David Provan, Davie Kinnear (Trainer).

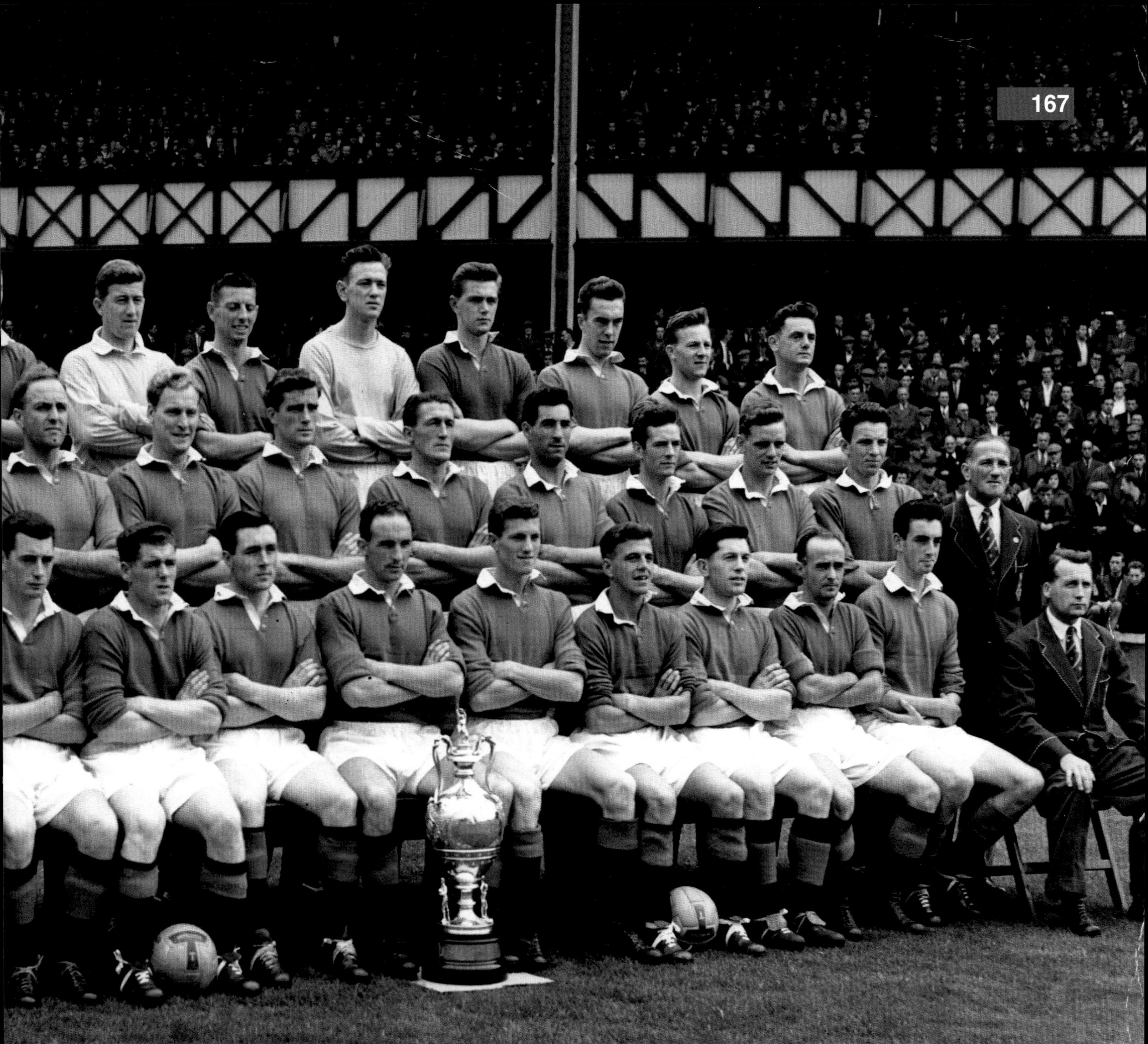

1959

■ **Rangers Football Club 1959-60.**

The Rangers won the Scottish Cup, so it wasn't a failure of a domestic season. But the real breakthrough was deep progression in Europe. Rangers made it to the semi-final of the European Cup before meeting an in-form Eintracht Frankfurt side.

Incredibly, despite taking a 6-1 reverse in the away leg, more than 70,000 came to Ibrox for the second leg.

Back, from left: George Duncan, Stewart McCorquodale, John Queen, Willie Cassidy, Alan Austin, Norrie Martin, George Niven, Billy Ritchie, Alexander Brooks, Bobby Orr, Roger Hynd, Max Murray, Hugh Neill, John Little.

Middle: Jimmy Millar, Alexander Gold, Willie Stevenson, Bobby King, Ian McColl, Tom Dawson, Sammy Baird, George McLean, Bill Paterson, Bobby Grant, Harold Davis, Ron McKinnon, David Provan, Thomas McKechnie, Willie Telfer, Joe Craven (assistant trainer).

Front: Scot Symon (manager), Ralph Brand, Robert McCallum, Alex Scott, John Currie, Ian McMillan, Billy Stark, Bobby Shearer, Bobby Hume, Eric Caldow, Bobby Brown, Brian McIlroy, Davie Wilson, Davie Kinnear (trainer).

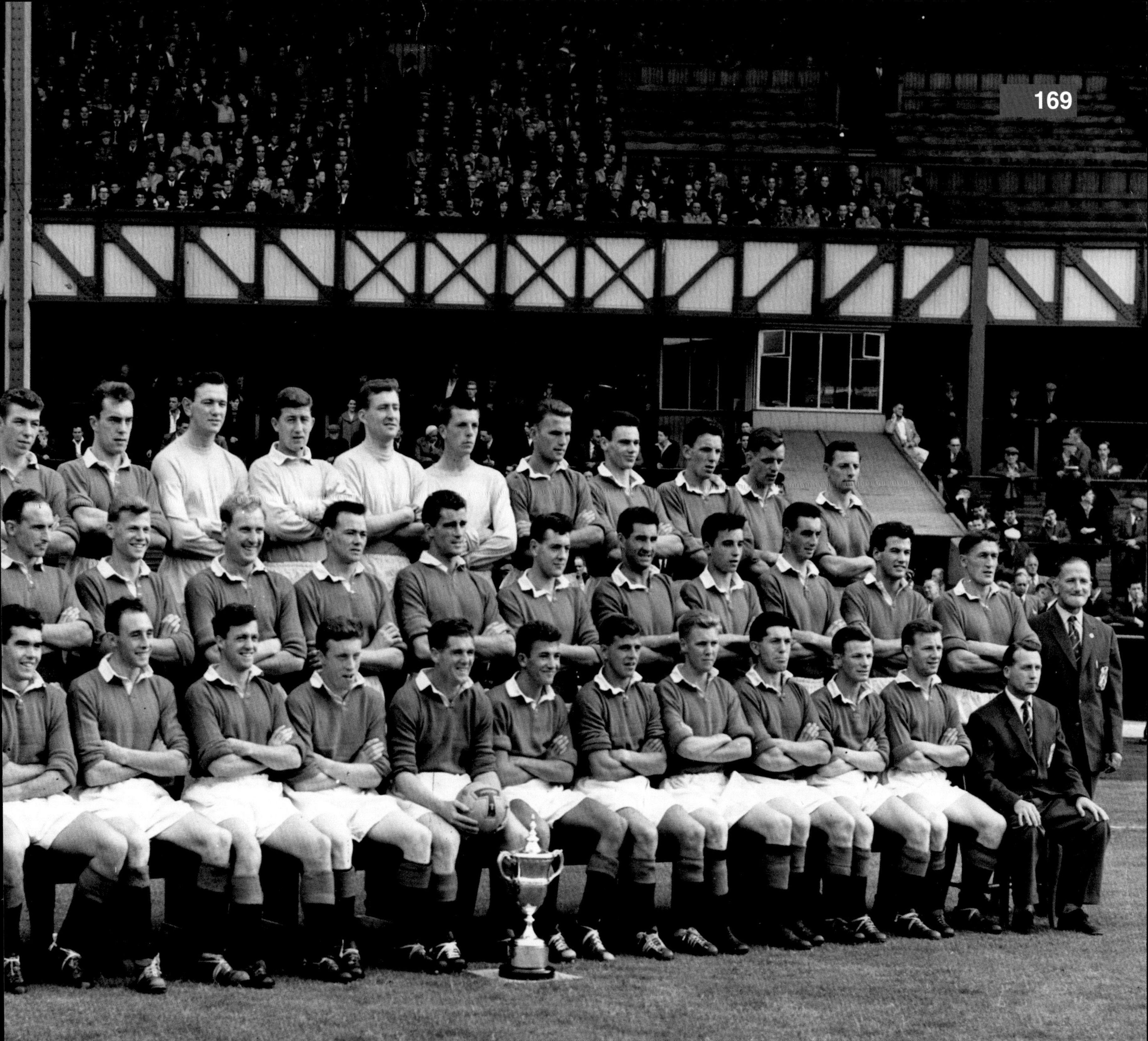

1960

■ **Rangers FC 1960-61.**

With Jim Baxter (see also page 112) now in the ranks this was a superb Rangers team, full of goals.

The League and League Cup were won, and The Rangers then became the first British team to reach a European final, beating England's much-admired Wolverhampton Wanderers side in the semi.

They went down, over two legs, in the Cup Winners' Cup Final to a street-wise, play-acting, shirt-tugging Fiorentina.

Back, from left: Stan Anderson, Jimmy Millar, John Currie, Bobby Hume, Ron McKinnon, Norrie Martin, George Niven, Billy Ritchie, Bobby Grant, Max Murray, Willie Penman, Andy Matthew, Willie Henderson, Ralph Brand,

Middle: Scot Symon (manager), Albert Franks, Reuben Evans, Willie Stevenson, David More, Sammy Baird, George McLean, Bill Paterson, Bobby King, Harry Davis, Roger Hynd, Willie Telfer, Dave Provan, Jim Baxter, Joe Craven (assistant trainer).

Front: Alex Scott, Willie Cassidy, Ian McMillan, John Queen, Bobby Shearer, Billy Young, Eric Caldow, Donald Bowie, Ian McColl, Craig Brown, John Little, Craig Watson, Davie Wilson, Davie Kinnear (trainer).

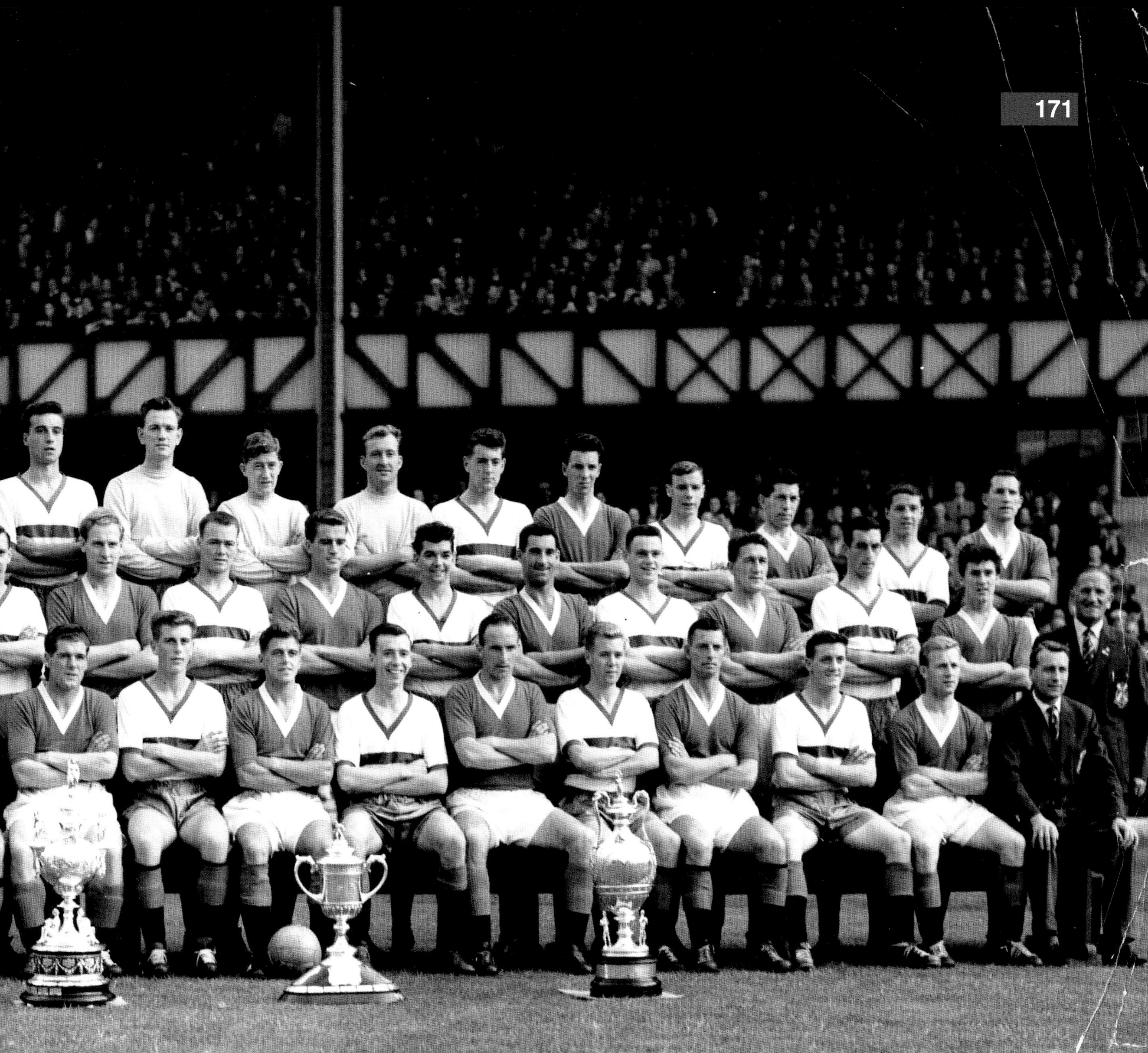

1962

■ **Rangers Football Club 1962-63.**

Ready for one of the most dominant seasons since the war. This was a team of iron and artistry in equal measure – a team Mr Struth himself would have been proud to lead. The championship would be won by nine points, the most comfortable margin since the equally powerful 1938-39 team.

Back, from left: Willie Henderson, Wilson Wood, Willie Penman, Michael Neil, George McLean, Norrie Martin, Ken McFarlane, George Niven, Max Murray, Willie Hunter, Bobby Hume, Bobby Burnside, Johnny Little.

Middle: Albert Franks, Ian Binnie, Willie Stevenson, Bobby King, Ronnie McKinnon, David More, Bill Paterson, Reuben Evans, Doug Baillie, Bobby Sutherland, Harry Davis, Roger Hynd, Davie Provan, John Greenwood, Jim Baxter, Cliff Reid, Stan Anderson, Joe Craven (assistant trainer).

Front: Scot Symon (manager), Alex Scott, Craig Watson, Jim Christie, Alec Willoughby, Bobby Shearer, George Mooney, Eric Caldow, John Greig, Jimmy Millar, Jim Forrest, Ralph Brand, Sammy Wilson, Davie Wilson, Davie Kinnear (trainer).

1963

■ **Rangers Football Club 1963-64.**

Triple Crown winners for the second time in the club's history.

This Rangers team was majestic – strong, entertaining, and resilient, with the winning combination of a mean defence and potent attack.

Great Rangers, every one.

Back, from left: Wilson Wood, Jim Forrest, Jim Christie, Craig Watson, Billy Ritchie, Ken McFarlane, Norrie Martin, Willie Hunter, Willie Mathieson, Ron McKinnon, Danny McLardy, Alec Willoughby.

Middle: David Marshall, John Greig, Mike Neil, Harold Davis, Bobby Sutherland, Doug Baillie, Roger Hynd, David Provan, Colin Jackson, George McLean, Bobby Watson, Jim Baxter, Jim Pickering Joe Craven (asst trainer).

Front: Scot Symon (manager), Willie Henderson, Billy McCartney, Ian McMillan, Dennis Setterington, Eric Caldow, George Mooney, Bobby Shearer, Alan Thomson, Jimmy Millar, Bobby Burnside, Ralph Brand, Derek Traill, Davie Wilson, Davie Kinnear (physio).

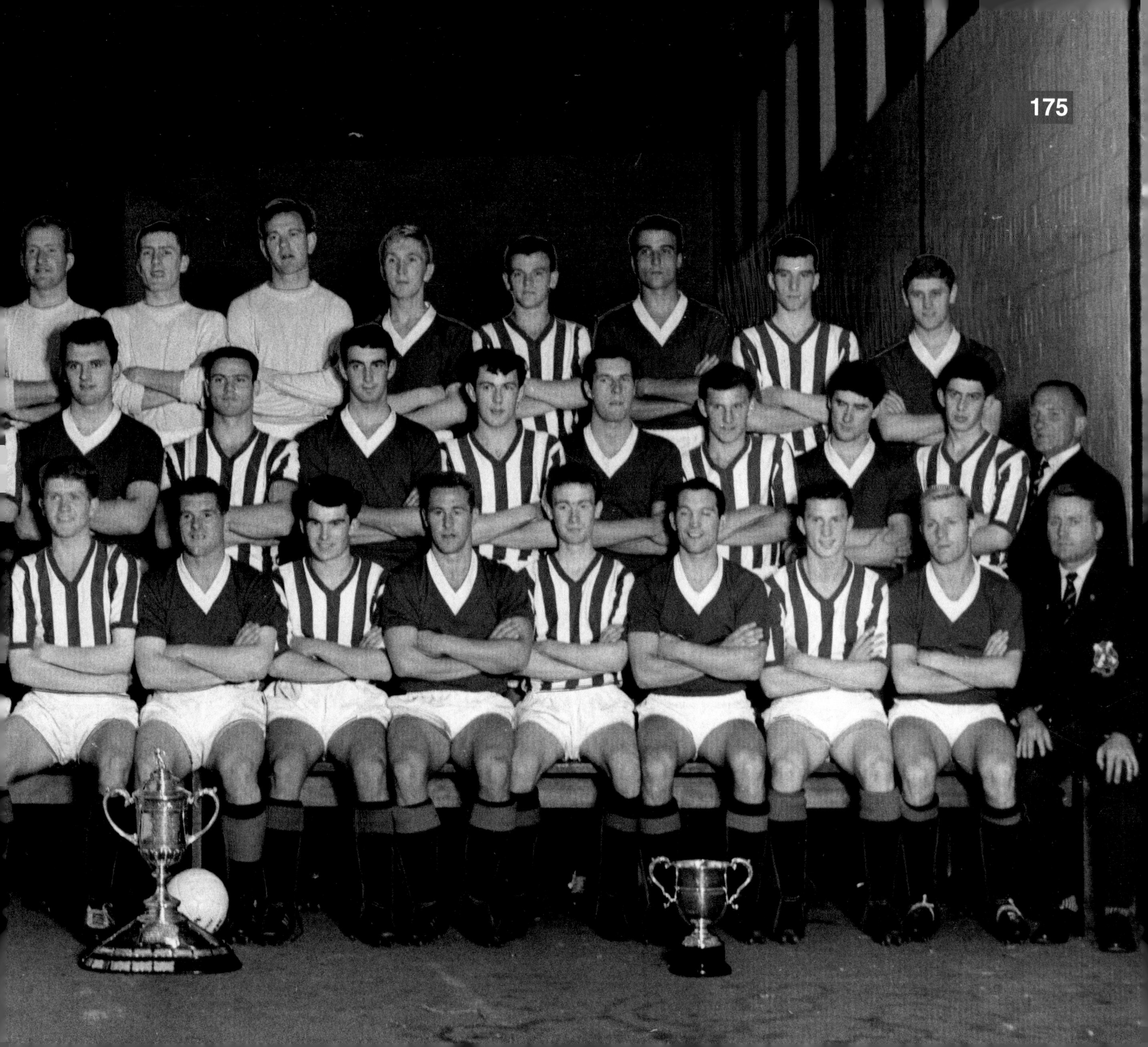

So how were these fascinating, and regimented, team photos taken?

One of the main men to thank is Bob Wilson, for many years Rangers' official photographer.

He set up pre-season press events, and arranged the players in place. This may sound simple, but to achieve the level of consistency, and quality, exhibited in Rangers photos was no easy task. Others tried to recreate the majesty of a Rangers team line-up, but few came close.

But Bob wasn't just a photographer. He had been a very good footballer, captaining Giffnock North to win the Scottish Amateur Cup in 1957.

After a knee injury ended his career he rose to be a Grade 1 referee, after a suggestion by the most famous ref of the era, Tom "Tiny" Wharton, that he take up a whistle.

■ **Here is Bob bringing his equipment out and leading the way across the pitch for a 1964 photo taken before a public trial match. Here and overleaf, he places the trophies and composes the team – and the rest of the photographers – the way he wants them.**

■ Almost ready, right, hold it like that . . .

1964

■ **Rangers Football Club 1964.**

This is the 43 players who made up the 1963-64 Triple Crown squad. It is the photo that Bob took such pains to set up to his exact requirements on the previous page. It was taken before a Monday evening trial match on August 3rd, 1964.

Back, from left: Wilson Wood, Willie Mathieson, Craig Watson, Jim Stewart, Bobby Watson, Ian Binnie, Norrie Martin, Billy Ritchie, Ken McFarlane, Tom Donnelly, Jim Forrest, George Mooney, Alec Willoughby, Alex Reid, Derek Traill

Middle: Billy McCartney, John Greig, Richard Moir, Ron McKinnon, Colin Jackson, Roger Hynd, Jimmy Simpson, Doug Baillie, Dave Ritchie, Davie Provan, Bobby Sutherland, George McLean, Bobby King, Jim Baxter, Danny McLardy, Joe Craven (assistant trainer)

Front: Scot Symon (manager), Willie Henderson, Willie Johnstone, Ian McMillan, Denis Setterington, Eric Caldow, William Smith, Bobby Shearer, Alan Thomson, Jimmy Millar, Billy Semple, Ralph Brand, John Vint, Davie Wilson, Davie Kinnear (trainer).

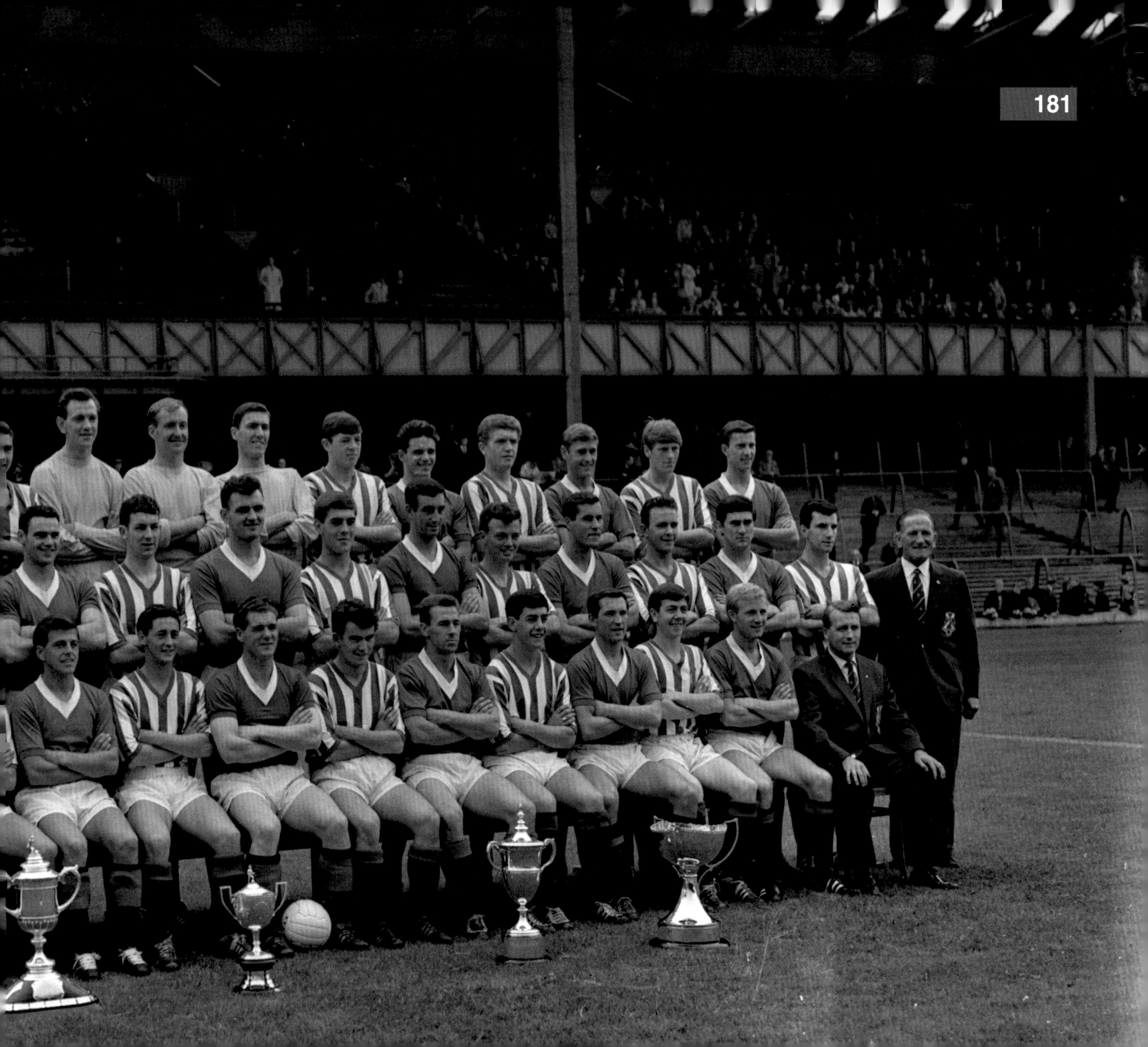

1964

■ **Rangers Football Club, 1964-65.**

This team won the League Cup, but it was to be a season in which Hearts, Dunfermline and (the ultimate winners) Kilmarnock fought out the League title.

Rangers had a great side, and needed such greatness in the decades after the war. There was probably no other era in Scottish football history in which the challenge for trophies came from so many good teams.

Rangers dominated this era, of course. Rangers, as Mr Struth would have told you, are made for challenges.

Back, from left: Bobby Shearer, Eric Caldow, David Provan, Billy Ritchie, John Greig, Ron McKinnon, Jim Baxter.
Front: Scot Symon (manager), Willie Henderson, Ian McMillan, George McLean, Jimmy Millar, Jim Forrest, Ralph Brand, Davie Wilson, Davie Kinnear (trainer).

1965

■ **Rangers Football Club 1965-66.**

The mid-1960s to mid-1970s are often seen as a dark time for Rangers, but this isn't entirely true. Though they did not win a championship for a decade, Rangers produced some excellent players and very potent teams.

Never did they fall far down the league, or stop being one of the greatest clubs in Britain. Rangers are always Rangers, they can never be written off, never be taken lightly.

Back, from left: Alec Willoughby, James Stewart, Craig Watson, Bill Paterson, Bobby Watson, Findlay McGillivray, Billy Ritchie, Norrie Martin, Ken McFarlane, Danny McLardy, Tottie Beck, Sandy Jardine, Willie Mathieson, William Smith, Derek Traill.

Middle: Kai Johansen, Tom Donnelly, John Greig, Colin Jackson, Ron McKinnon, David Ritchie, David Provan, Jimmy Simpson, Roger Hynd, Bobby Sutherland, George McLean, Billy McCartney, Wilson Wood, Joe Craven (assistant trainer).

Front: Scot Symon (manager), Willie Henderson, Billy Paul, Jimmy Millar, Alex Reid, Jim Forrest, Dennis Setterington, Eric Caldow, Billy Semple, Ralph Brand, Jim Jardine, Willie Johnston, John Vint, Davie Wilson, Davie Kinnear (trainer).

1967

■ **Rangers Football Club 1967.**

A damaged photo in the last few months of Scot Symon's reign, of what was a damaged team with the infamous loss to Berwick. But this wasn't a bad side by any means. They narrowly lost the title, and had reached the League Cup and Cup Winners' Cup Finals. Not bad by other clubs' standards, But Rangers' expectations are higher than other clubs.

Back, from left: Tom Donnelly, Alex Smith, James Ferguson, Eric Sorensen, Norrie Martin, Billy Ritchie, Ken McFarlane, Willie Sutherland.
Middle: Alex Paterson, Bobby Watson, Alex Miller, Davie Provan, Rikki Fleming, Ron McKinnon, Colin Jackson, Roger Hynd, Billy Miller, Dave Smith, Willie Mathieson, Kai Johansen, Cammy Evans, Sandy Jardine, Joe Craven (coach).
Front: Scot Symon (manager), Davie White (assistant manager), Willie Henderson (obscured), Billy Paul, Alec Willoughby, Billy Semple, Alex Ferguson, Jim Jardine, John Greig, Dennis Setterington, Andy Penman, Alex Reid, Willie Johnston, Davie Kinnear (trainer), Bobby Seith (coach).

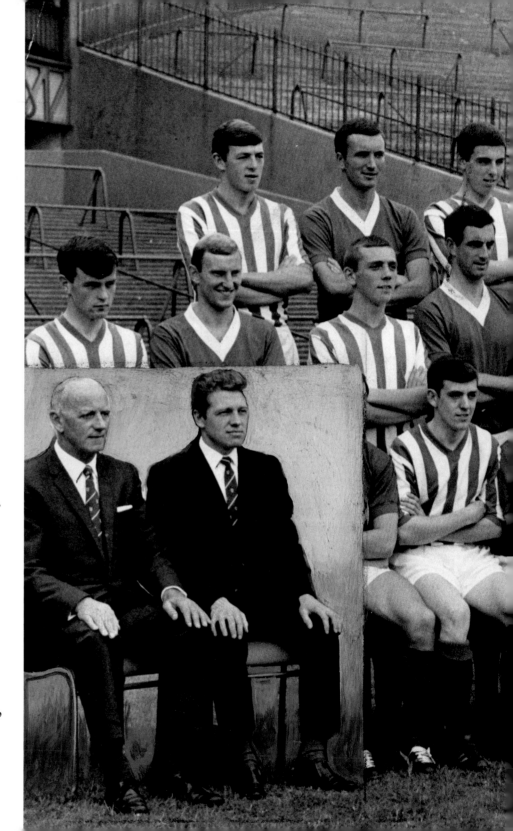

1968

■ **Rangers Football Club 1968-69.**

The new crew-necked jerseys looked good, and the team played some good-looking football under Davie White. But this was a barren season.

A lack of trophies is something that will not be tolerated for long at Ibrox.

Back, from left: Alex Smith, Willie White, Colin Jackson, Alex Stirling, Eric Sorensen, Norrie Martin, Murray McDermott, Graham Keddie, Orjan Persson, Alfie Conn, Willie Mathieson.

Middle: Laurie Smith (physiotherapist), Bobby Watson, Ken Watson, David Provan, Wilson Wood, Ron McKinnon, Jimmy Johnstone, Roger Hynd, Alex Miller, Dave Smith, David Cairns, Kai Johansen, Cammy Evans, Sandy Jardine.

Front: Davie Kinnear (trainer), Willie Henderson, Billy Laing, Alec Willoughby, Dennis Setterington, Alex Ferguson, Davie White (manager), John Greig, Billy McPhee, Andy Penman, Brian Heron, Billy Semple, Joe Craven (assistant trainer).

1969

■ **Rangers Football Club 1969.**

Jim Baxter had returned, and this team features Scotland's first £100,000 player, Colin Stein. But, again, it won no silverware.

Davie White would be replaced as manager before the end of November.

Back, from left: David Provan, Gus McCallum, Colin Jackson, Graham Keddie, Eric Sorensen, Norrie Martin, Gerry Neef, Danny Stevenson, Dennis Setterington, Jim Baxter, Norrie Stevenson, Alex Ferguson, Iain McDonald,

Middle: Laurie Smith (physiotherapist), Bobby Watson, Ken Watson, Willie Mathieson, Tom Matchett, Ron McKinnon, Jimmy Millar, Orjan Persson, David Cairns, Dave Smith, Graham Fyfe, Kai Johansen, Billy Semple, Sandy Jardine, Joe Craven (assistant trainer).

Front: Davie White (manager), Willie Henderson, Billy Laing, Alex MacDonald, Alfie Conn, Colin Stein, Willie White, John Greig, Billy McPhee, Andy Penman, Brian Heron, Willie Johnston, Willie Thornton (assistant manager), Davie Kinnear (trainer).

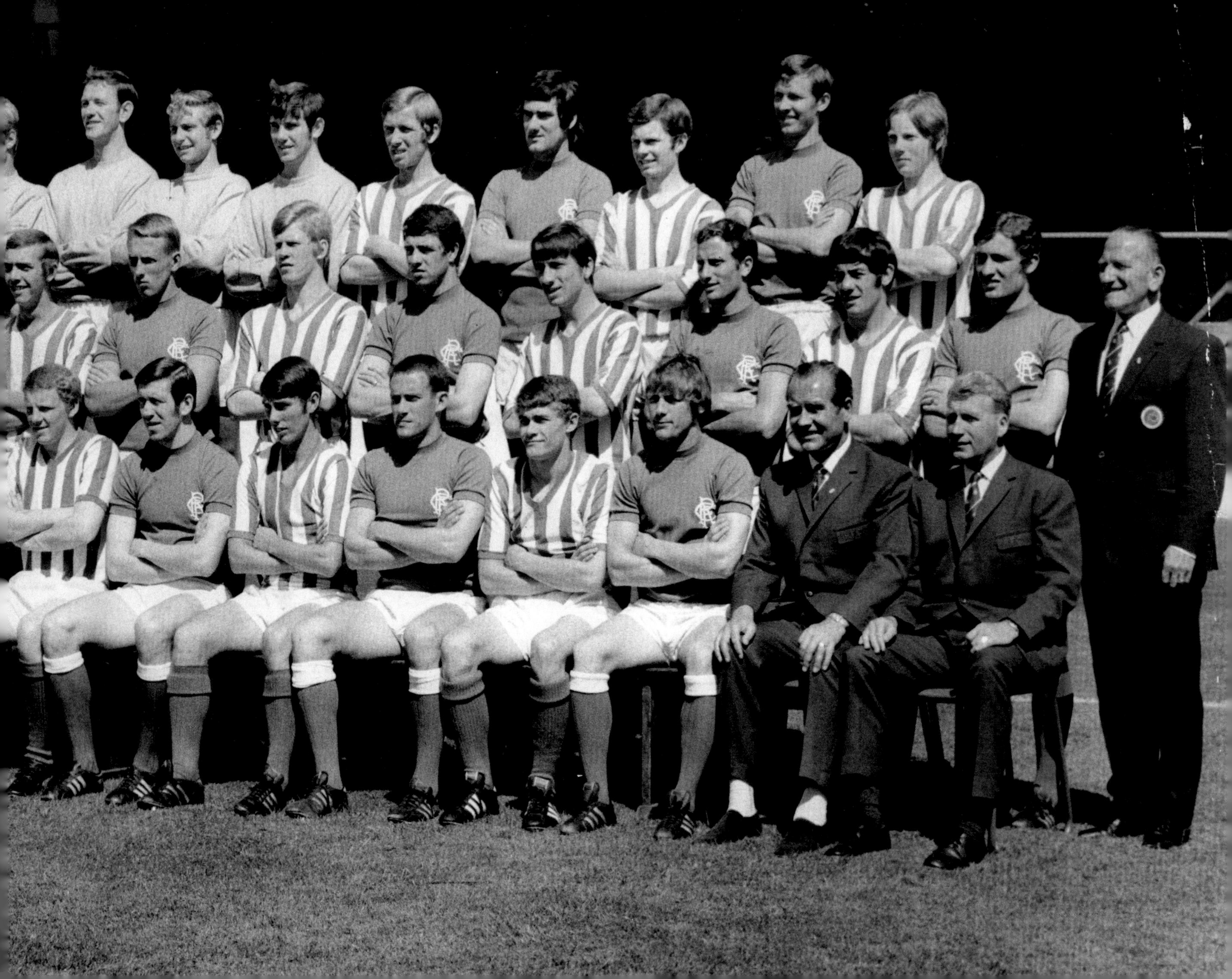

1970

■ **Rangers Football Club 1970.**

Quite a change in personnel from the previous year. A new man in charge in Willie Waddell, with his trainer-coach Jock Wallace. The fitness of the players was taken to new levels, and some of the men shown here were to go on to be great Rangers men.

Indeed, with the new decade, the foundations of a new era were being put in place.

Back, from left: Alfie Conn, Colin Stein, George Donaldson, Gerry Neef, Peter McCloy, Colin Jackson, Bobby Watson, Danny Stevenson, Graham Fyfe, Iain MacDonald.

Middle: Jock Wallace (trainer-coach), Tom Craig (physiotherapist), Ken Watson, Willie Mathieson, Derek Renton, Ron McKinnon, Alex Miller, Sandy Jardine, Derek Johnstone, Dave Smith, Gus McCallum, Joe Craven (assistant trainer), Stan Anderson (assistant coach).

Front: Willie Waddell (manager), Willie Henderson, Billy Semple, Alex MacDonald, Tom Alexander, John Greig, Derek Parlane, Andy Penman, Alex Morrison, Willie Johnston, Willie Thornton (assistant manager).

1971

■ **Rangers Football Club 1971.**

After four years, silverware returns to the Rangers pre-season line-up photo, thanks to young Derek Johnstone's aerial prowess in the League Cup Final.

Tommy McLean was signed from Kilmarnock, Peter McLoy became the first-choice keeper, and Sandy Jardine established himself as a full-back.

A great team was taking shape.

Back, from left: George Struthers, Alfie Conn, Graham Fyfe, Colin Jackson, Gerry Neef, Peter McCloy, Bobby Watson, Derek Johnstone, George Donaldson, Alex Miller, Iain McDonald,
Middle: Jock Wallace (coach), Tom Craig (physiotherapist), Colin Stein, Neil Pirrie, Willie Mathieson, Jim Denny, Ronnie McKinnon, Gus McCallum, Sandy Jardine, Andy Penman, Dave Smith, George Walker, Stan Anderson (assistant coach); Joe Craven (trainer).
Front: Willie Waddell (manager), Willie Henderson, Billy Semple, Alex MacDonald, Tom Alexander, John Greig, Derek Parlane, Tommy McLean, Alex Morrison, Willie Johnston, Willie Thornton (assistant manager).

1973

■ **Rangers Football Club 1973.**

There is a determination building in The Rangers. This team had memorably won the Scottish Cup, with Tom Forsyth's pile-driver, in the last final in Scotland that would ever be played in front of a six-figure crowd.

But the forthcoming 1973-74 season would be trophy-less again. This just could not be allowed to continue.

Back, from left: Dave Young, George Struthers, Ally Scott, Colin Jackson, Donald Hunter, Peter McCloy, Stewart Kennedy, Tom Forsyth, Derek Burke, George Donaldson, Billy McNicol.

Middle: Tom Craig (physiotherapist), Iain MacDonald, Johnny Hamilton, Alex O'Hara, Alfie Conn, Dave Smith, Derek Johnstone, Alex Miller, Ian Thomson, Willie Mathieson, Graham Fyfe, Ian McDougall, Stan Anderson (trainer).

Front: Jock Wallace (manager), Eric Morris, Tommy Mclean, Alex MacDonald, Doug Houston, Derek Parlane, John Greig, Sandy Jardine, Joe Mason, Billy Steele, Quinton Young, Jim Denny, Willie Thornton (assistant manager).

1974

■ **Rangers Football Club 1974-75.**

The return of the kings. The last 18-team First Division, and Rangers marked the occasion by storming to their first championship in a decade in fine style. There was flair and power in this team. Solid at the back with Greig, Forsyth and Jardine, industrious in midfield with MacDonald and Young, and the wizardy of McLean fed the devastating duo of Johnstone and Parlane.

Back, from left: Dave Smith, Martin Henderson, Tom Forsyth, Colin Jackson, Stewart Kennedy, Peter McCloy, Donald Hunter, Ally Scott, Alfie Conn, Derek Parlane, Richard Sharp.
Middle: Willie Mathieson, Gordon Boyd, Chris Robertson, Davy Armour, Alex Miller, Derek Johnstone, Johnny Hamilton, Isaac Farrell, Alex O'Hara, Billy McNicol, Joe Mason (assistant trainer);
Front: Jock Wallace (manager), Jim Denny, Eric Morris, Graham Fyfe, Ian McDougall, John Greig, Alex MacDonald, Billy Steele, Tommy McLean, Quinton Young, Tom Craig (physiotherapist).

1975

■ **Rangers Football Club 1975.**

This team would be Treble winners, The Rangers in their rightful, and expected, place.

This team conceded just 24 goals in that 36-game 1975-76 season. They were stronger, faster, fitter, more confident, and more determined than all other teams – and they could play a bit, too.

Back, from left: Colin Stein, Derek Parlane, Colin Jackson, Donald Hunter, Peter McCloy, Stewart Kennedy, Ally Scott, Tom Forsyth, Martin Henderson.
Middle: Tom Craig (physiotherapist), Gordon Boyd, Chris Robertson, Alex O'Hara, Alan Boyd, Derek Johnstone, Alex Miller, Ally Dawson, Davy Armour, Ian McDougall, Joe Mason (trainer);
Front: Jock Wallace (manager), Tommy McLean, Bobby McKean, Graham Fyfe, Alex MacDonald, John Greig, Sandy Jardine, Quinton Young, Eric Morris, Jim Denny, Johnny Hamilton.

1976

■ **Rangers Football Club 1976.**

Surprisingly, given the previous season's dominance, this would be a quiet year for Jock's Rangers, without silverware.

There was more to come from this team, though.

Back, from left: Alex Miller, Derek Parlane, Martin Henderson, Stewart Kennedy, Peter McCloy, Ronnie Lowrie, Colin Jackson, Kenny Watson, Tom Forsyth.

Middle: Tom Craig, Ian McDougall, Ralph Brand, Chris Robertson, Colin Stein, Derek Johnstone, Alan Boyd, Davy Armour, Alex O'Hara, Ally Dawson, Joe Mason (trainer).

Front: Jock Wallace (manager), Tommy McLean, Gordon Boyd, Eric Morris, Sandy Jardine, John Greig, Jim Denny, Alex MacDonald, Bobby McKean, Iain Munro, Johnny Hamilton.

1977

■ **Rangers Football Club 1977.**

Another glorious treble-winning team, with world-class ability in the shape of new arrivals Davie Cooper and Bobby Russell.

They added star-quality to an already formidable footballing machine, and The Rangers would sweep all before them again.

Back, from left: Alan Boyd, Alex Miller, Derek Parlane, Colin Jackson, Ronnie Lowrie, Peter McCloy, Stewart Kennedy, Martin Henderson, Tom Forsyth, Kenny Watson.

Middle: Tom Craig, Gordon Boyd, Eric Morris, Ralph Brand, Chris Robertson, Derek Johnstone, Colin Stein, Davy Armour, Alex O'Hara, Jim Denny, Joe Mason.

Front: Billy MacKay, Tommy McLean, Iain Munro, Robert Russell, Sandy Jardine, John Greig, Davie Cooper, Alex MacDonald, Bobby McKean, Johnny Hamilton, Derek Strickland.

1978

■ **Rangers Football Club 1978.**

It had been a close season of momentous backroom change at Ibrox.

Another treble had been won by what was clearly the best squad of players in the country, but on Tuesday, May 23rd, Jock Wallace shocked Scottish football by resigning. John Greig, the very next day, moved straight from being captain on the pitch to the manager's office.

The playing staff who had marched to the Treble, however, saw just a few additions.

Back, from left: Alex Miller, Derek Parlane, Colin Jackson, Peter McCloy, Stewart Kennedy, Tom Forsyth, Kenny Watson, Alan Boyd.

Middle: Tom Craig (physio), Eric Morris, Stephen Richardson, Ralph Brand, Derek Johnstone, Gordon Smith, Davy Armour, Ally Dawson, Jim Denny, Joe Mason (trainer).

Front: John Greig (manager), Billy MacKay, Chris Robertson, Tommy McLean, Sandy Jardine, John MacDonald, Davie Cooper, Alex MacDonald, Bobby Russell, Derek Strickland.

1979

■ **Rangers Football Club 1979.**

John Greig achieved the remarkable feat of winning the League and Scottish Cups in his debut season as a manager.

But John had inherited an ageing team, and there was a high level of expenditure on rebuilding three sides of Ibrox.

Back, from left: Alex Forsyth, Alex Miller, Derek Parlane, Stephen Richardson, Colin Jackson, Peter McCloy, Stewart Kennedy, Ray McIntosh, Tom Forsyth, Kenny Watson, Ross McLaren.

Middle: Stan Anderson (assistant coach), Chris Robertson, Iain Stirton, Gordon Dalziel, Gordon Smith, Davy Armour, Ally Dawson, Jim Denny, Billy Urquhart, Derek Matthew, Eric Morris.

Front: John Greig (manager), Billy MacKay, Tommy McLean, Derek Strickland, Sandy Jardine, Derek Johnstone, Davie Cooper, Alex MacDonald, Bobby Russell, John MacDonald, Tom Craig (physio), Joe Mason (trainer).

1980

■ **Rangers Football Club 1980.**

This Rangers side won the Scottish Cup in what would come to be known as: "The Davie Cooper Final".

At this point in his career an in-form Cooper was probably the best footballer in Britain.

Back, from left: Iain Stirton, Gregor Stevens, Colin Jackson, Colin McAdam, George Young, Peter McCloy, Gordon Marshall, Ray McIntosh, Tom Forsyth, Kenny Watson, Robert Clark.

Middle: David Provan (chief scout), Stan Anderson (trainer), Graham Watson, Kenny Lyall, Alex Miller, Stephen Richardson, Ian Redford, Jim Bett, Billy Urquhart, Gordon Dalziel, Dougie Robertson, Alex Forsyth, Tom Craig (physiotherapist);

Front: John Greig (manager), Billy Davies, Tommy McLean, John MacDonald, Sandy Jardine, Derek Johnstone, Davie Cooper, Bobby Russell, Alex MacDonald, Billy MacKay, Joe Mason (trainer).

1981

■ **Rangers Football Club 1981.**

The new Ibrox was finally ready, with the opening of the Govan Stand marking the last stage of the transition from old-fashioned bowl-type ground to one of the finest stadiums in Europe.

This team captured the League Cup.

Back, from left: Tom Forsyth, Robert Clark, Colin McAdam, John McClelland, Peter McCloy, Jim Stewart, Gordon Marshall, Dave McPherson, Colin Jackson, Gregor Stevens, Alex Miller.

Middle: David Provan (chief scout), Stan Anderson (coach), Jim McIntyre, Graham Watson, Gordon Dalziel, Ian Redford, Derek Johnstone, Jim Bett, Dougie Robertson, Kenny Lyall, Alex Forsyth, Kenny Black, Stuart Hogg (sprint coach), Tom Craig (physiotherapist).

Front: John Greig (manager), Tommy McLean, Billy MacKay, Billy Davies, Bobby Russell, Ally Dawson, Sandy Jardine, Davie Cooper, John MacDonald, Willie Johnston, Joe Mason (trainer).

1982

■ **Rangers Football Club 1982.**

The Rangers of this era had a squad of good individual players, but failed to really impress as a team despite reaching both of the season's major cup finals.

Back, from left: Andrew Kennedy, John McClelland, Dave McPherson, Colin McAdam, Andy Bruce, Jim Stewart, Peter McCloy, Gordon Marshall, Craig Paterson, Gregor Stevens, Alex Miller, Kenny Lyall.
Middle: Stan Anderson (second team coach), Jim McIntyre, Bobby Russell, Willie Muir, Ian Redford, Dougie Robertson, Jim Bett, Eric Ferguson, Dave MacKinnon, Kenny Black, Stuart Hogg (sprint coach), Bob Findlay (physiotherapist).
Front: John Greig (manager); Tommy McLean (assistant manager), John MacDonald, Andy Willock, Derek Johnstone, Billy MacKay, Ally Dawson, Gordon Dalziel, Davie Cooper, Billy Davies, Robert Prytz, Joe Mason (second team coach), David Provan (youth coach).

1983

■ **Rangers Football Club 1983.**

A young man named Alistair Murdoch McCoist arrived from Sunderland just before this photo was taken, adding much-needed finishing power to the team.

He marked his first season with a superb hat-trick in the League Cup Final.

But during this season the great John Greig left the club, allowing Jock Wallace to become the first man to manage Rangers twice.

The team photos had, by this time, changed a great deal from those that had been taken in earlier decades.

Back, from left: Dave MacKinnon, Ally Dawson, Ally McCoist, Robert Prytz,
Middle: Ian Redford, Gregor Stevens, Craig Paterson, Peter McCloy, Dave McPherson, Sandy Clark, Davie Cooper.
Front: Kenny Lyall, John McDonald, John McClelland, Billy Davies, Bobby Russell.

■ **Rangers Football Club 1984.**

A League Cup would be taken this season, and there was a return to something like the old style of Rangers photos.

Back, from left: Robert Prytz, Derek Ferguson, David MacFarlane, Andrew Kennedy, David McPherson, John McClelland, Craig Paterson, Colin McAdam, David Mitchell, Eric Ferguson, Stuart Munro, Robert Fleck.

Middle: Stan Anderson (coach), Colin Lindsay, Billy

1984

Davies, Iain Durrant, Scott Fraser, Nicky Walker, Peter McCloy, Andy Bruce, Hugh Burns, David MacKinnon, Tom Leeman, Steven Connors, Bob Findlay (physio). Front: Ian Redford, Ally Dawson, Iain Ferguson,

Bobby Williamson, Davie Cooper, Alex Totten (coach), Jock Wallace (manager), John Hagart (coach), Sandy Clark, Cammy Fraser, Ally McCoist, Robert Russell, John MacDonald.

1985

■ **Rangers Football Club 1985.**

Fifth place in the League and an easy touch in the cups is not good enough for The Rangers.

Things could not be allowed to go on. A revolution was required, and an incredible one was about to come.

But that is such a huge story that it will take another book to tell.

Back, from left: David MacKinnon; Stuart Munro, David MacFarlane, Scott Nisbet, David McPherson, Craig Paterson, Eric Ferguson, Stuart Beattie, Alistair Dawson, Derek Ferguson.

Middle: Robert Prytz, Iain Durrant; Cammy Fraser, Ted McMinn, Andy Bruce, Peter McCloy, Nicky Walker, Derek Johnstone, Hugh Burns, Billy Davies, Colin Miller.

Front: Stan Anderson (coach), John MacDonald, Iain Ferguson, Bobby Williamson, Davie Cooper, Alex Totten (assistant manager), Jock Wallace (manager), John Hagart (coach), Bobby Russell, Ally McCoist, Ian Redford, Robert Fleck, Bob Findlay (physio).

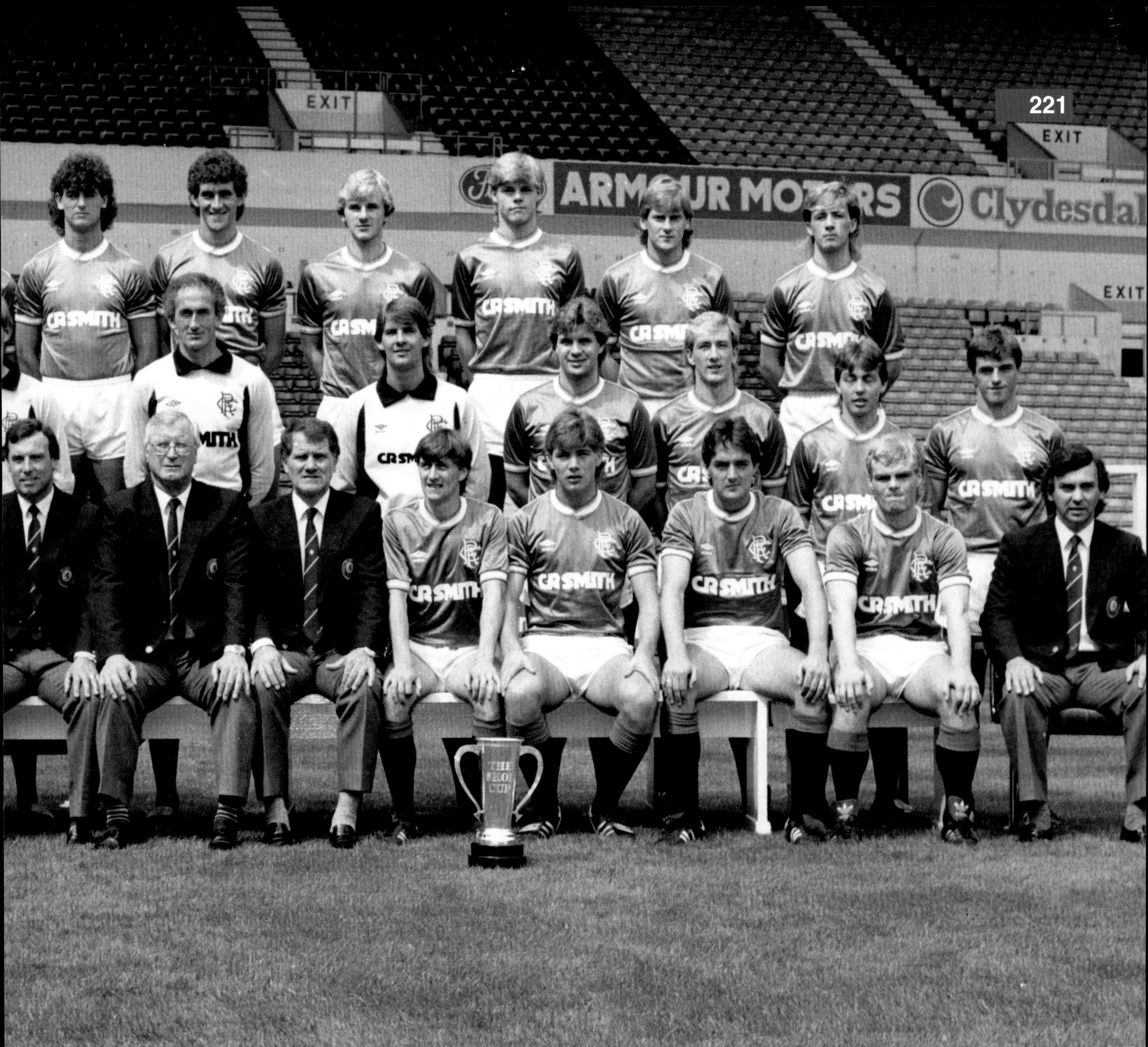
EXIT
EXIT
EXIT
ARMOUR MOTORS
Clydesdal
CR SMITH

Just a boy's game

RANGERS' history is filled with players who were taken from smaller clubs and given a chance to prove themselves a Rangers man. .

Indeed, playing well when competing against Rangers is a well-trodden route to the Ibrox players' entrance – which is a double-edged sword. Players of other clubs know that if they show up well in a game, especially a game at Ibrox, then they have a chance of a transfer bid being made for their services. This makes them try harder when playing against Rangers.

However, Rangers players are used to other clubs upping their game. True Rangers men cope with this. Overall, the system works well.

Many players would tell you that being selected for Rangers is better than being selected for their national side. They get to be a Rangers player every day.

In the past, methods of recruitment were different. It wasn't unusual for promising youngsters to be plucked from the Junior game in their teenage years, or even early 20s, and quickly make it to the first team.

Some, of course, came through the ranks at Rangers, although the system of youth football in the black and white era was vastly different to the highly-coached academies system of today. Perhaps it is better these days, perhaps not.

All of them started as fresh-faced youths, with everything before them and everything to gain.

■ **Left: Alex Ferguson as a laddie at Dunfermline. He could have had a great career at Ibrox, might even have one day been made manager. But he blew his chance.**

■ Left: An 18-year-old Colin Jackson in 1964.
■ Above: Tommy McLean (aged 15) in 1963, in his Scotland Schoolboys team blazer.

■ **Right:** November 8th, 1941, a wartime league game against Hamilton Accies at the old Douglas Park that saw a gangly 19-year-old named George Young make his Rangers debut.

■ **Far left:** Davie Cooper in 1977, just before he signed for Rangers.

■ **Middle Left:** January 1971. Derek Johnstone playing for the Scottish schoolboys. He still qualified for the schools team, despite being an established Rangers regular and having scored a League Cup Final-winning goal.

■ **Near Left:** Willie Thornton, aged 16, on February 8th, 1937.

A football star while still at Broxburn School, Willie had just scored the first of his 188 goals for Rangers. His career was badly interrupted when Adolf Hitler stopped play two years later.

Willie served with the Scottish Horse during the war, winning the Military Medal for bravery.

A true Rangers man.

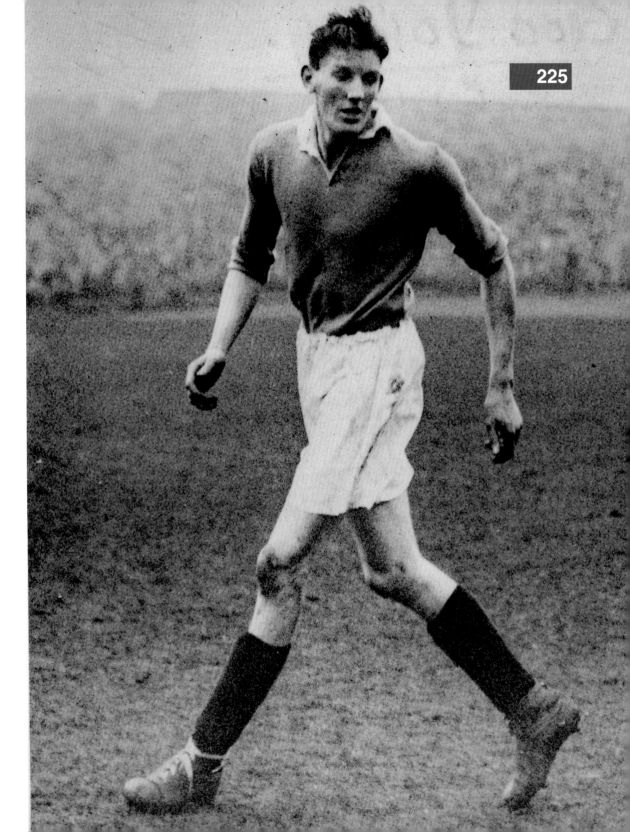

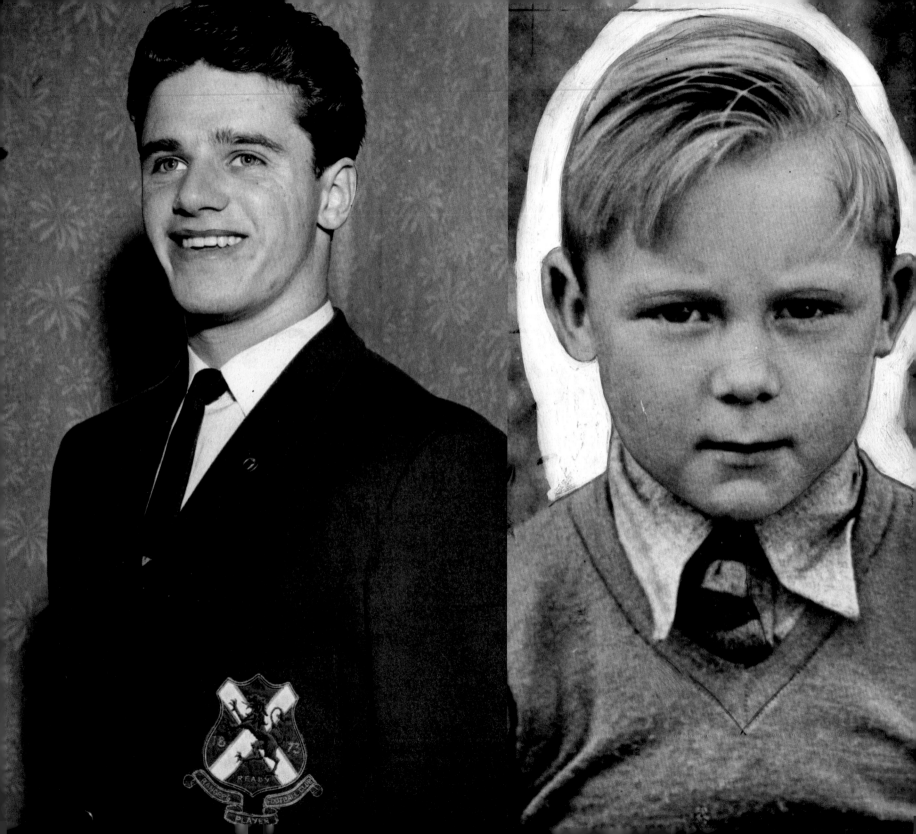

■ Ian McMillan, the "wee prime minister" at Airdrie in 1956.

■ Far left: Young Jim Forrest, resplendent in his Rangers blazer in 1964.

■ Left: There was always a wee glint of devilment in Willie Johnston's eye, even when he was a bairn.

■ Right: Willie Henderson in 1959. He was another who was a first-team player while still at school. And looks pleased about it.

■ John Greig as a wean playing in the middens (left), as a young scholar (above), and lining up for his youth team United Crossroads in Edinburgh (on the right). He signed for Rangers in 1961, and has remained a Rangers man ever since. Aye Ready.

■ Left: Tam Forsyth, when Jaws was just a minnow at Motherwell.

■ Above: Peter McLoy also started at Motherwell, before he grew to stand tall at Ibrox.

■ The very slim Jim
Baxter, aged 19, in
1959 while still at
Raith Rovers.

■ Sandy Jardine, looking like he'd prefer not to pose for a photo, on his debut v. Hearts on February 4th, 1967.

■ Ally McCoist, cutting a dash in his flares, when he was a promising young schoolboy footballer.

The greatest ever Ranger

TO be voted by supporters "the greatest ever Ranger" is quite something. Indeed to be placed foremost of the great names and great players of any football club is an admirable thing. But to be given the accolade at this club, with its long and proud history, is truly remarkable. John Greig has said he is slightly embarrassed by it, a measure of his character.

John truly is, and deserves to be, an icon of the nation's greatest footballing institution. But he is also an example of a rare type of person. He was a loyal servant to Rangers, a one-club man, a great leader, and, most importantly, he conducted himself with dignity and honour on the football field at all times.

The middle part of his career was a difficult era for the club but he consistently shone on the pitch. He was a superb footballer, the only Rangers captain to hold a European trophy above his head – and he played in that 1972 cup final while nursing along a stress fracture to a bone in his foot.

His modern day transfer value would be stratospheric, because captain John Greig transmitted his attitude to those around him. He made them all better players.

But off the park perhaps his stock rose even higher. He was revered as a man. He is respected by everyone in football – fans of all clubs, the greats of the game, and (most difficult of all) those who had lined up to play against him.

Football is designed to create rivalry and enmity between those who strive with every sinew to beat each other. Many a manager has warned his players that no matter what happens away from the pitch, while on it they have no friends.

Yet no former opponent has a bad word to say about John Greig.

He conducts himself impeccably. On every anniversary of the Ibrox Disaster of 1971 he lays a wreath at the plinth of the statue that bears his likeness and the names of the victims. And his dignity and sorrow at the time of the disaster set the tone for the way all the players faced and dealt with the horror.

Many years later, when Craig Whyte walked in the door, John Greig walked out, citing "lack of transparency" from the new man. John Greig wouldn't work with anyone he didn't feel had the best intentions for Rangers. He acted as a bellwether for how all Rangers supporters came to view the events of that time.

There are few men like him.

Make of the most of him. The world would be a vastly poorer place without examples of ability, honour and integrity such as John Greig MBE.

■ **The evening before Scotland v. West Germany in October 1969, John discusses the game with Billy Bremner and Jimmy Johnstone.**

■ February 1968, John is ready for a game on a pitch that would be declared unplayable today.

■ Tuesday, May 4th, 1976. John holds aloft the 1975-76 League trophy. The Ibrox crowd had just enjoyed a half-hour match played between the 1948 Treble winners and the 1964 Treble team. The "old timers" lined up:
1948: Brown, Rae, Shaw, McColl, Woodburn, Cox, Waddell, Finlay, Thornton, Duncanson, Rutherford.
1964: Ritchie, Shearer, Caldow, Provan, Baillie, Baxter, McLean, McMillan, Millar, Brand, Wilson.

■ This page: March 22, 1972. John leading The Rangers to victory in the home leg of the European Cup Winners' Cup Quarter-Final against Italian champions Torino.

■ Right: April 26th, 1975, John salutes the crowd at the celebrations upon winning the last First Division.

■ **Left: March 1967, John married Janette Graham.**

■ **Left: November 1977, John, Janette and son Murray at Buckingham Palace for the presentation of John's MBE for services to football.**

John was voted Scotland's player of the year in 1966, and 1976.

He was an inaugural inductee to the Scottish Football Hall of Fame, the Scottish Sports Hall of Fame, and the Rangers Hall of Fame.

He has five League Championship medals, six Scottish Cup winners medals, four League Cup winners medals, and one ECWC winners medal.

John was captain for 13 years. He played 755 games for Rangers and won 44 Scotland caps.

In 1999 he was voted by fans as The Greatest Ever Ranger.

■ John with the 1976 Scottish Cup, a 3-1 victory over Hearts. Above all else, John Greig was a winner. That is one of the main reasons he earned the title of greatest ever Ranger. It takes a special sort of stamina to win, and keep winning. His drive and determination are what set him apart.

■ For all his achievements, John would still tell you that the best part of being a footballer is spending every day kicking a fitba about with your mates.

A different world

THE world was a different place in the black and white era. Football was different, Ibrox was unrecognisable to what it is today, players were different, and newspapers reported on them in ways that will seem outlandish to modern eyes.

Full postal addresses for players printed in the newspapers? Digging the garden in shirt and tie (although sleeves were rolled up)?

Was it better back then? You'll have your own opinion on that.

Photographers were given access to some unusual, unsuspected activities that players would indulge in. Who would think of Bobby Shearer as a horseman, Derek Parlane as a gardener, or Alex Ferguson as a painter?

But in the black and white era players lived lives closer to those of the supporters. Rangers paid good salaries, by the standards of the time, but even top-class international stars were far from millionaires. They had jobs on the side, managed parenting without a phalanx of nannies, and their do-it-yourself was done by themselves. They were part of their communities.

It was, indeed, a different world.

■ **Left: Alex Scott polishes his tackety boots in 1958, while juggling his Rangers career with National Service in the Army.**

■ **This photo was taken in September 1950 and shows Ian McColl and Eddie Rutherford, Rangers team-mates and next-door-neighbours.**

It was printed in *The Sunday Post* and the caption gave the players' full addresses. Ian lived at 21 Maxwell Avenue, Ballieston, Eddie lived at No. 23.

The houses are still there – substantial, comfortable, and very nice semi-detached homes on a quiet, tree-lined street.

The photo shows them doing a spot of gardening, and the caption quips that they had stopped work for a chat over the fence – and were talking about football.

Few footballers have their full addresses printed in newspapers these days. Equally few get out in shirt and tie to dig their garden.

■ 1968. No one gave a second thought to showing off John Greig's new car, number plate and all, in the newspapers. Looks like a Rover P6 2000. Good set of wheels.

■ Colin Jackson in 1967, with an even more impressive ride.

George Niven was all set for a quiet, relaxing Christmas – until Santa brought a drum each for his young twins.

■ August 1967. Rangers' new £65,000 striker Alex Ferguson gives the steps of his house a lick of paint.

■ The public-spirited Ronnie McKinnon clearing the pavement in front of his house after a snowfall in January 1970. For reasons unknown, he brought wife Liz, and young child, with him!

■ Just as well she loves you Ronnie, when you look like that! Liz and Ronnie, with a badly broken nose suffered on March 18th, 1967, at Ayr United.

■ Goalie Billy Ritchie, outstanding in the great Rangers team of the early Sixties, was known as the quiet man of that team. But, seen here with wife Margaret and children in 1965, he must have spoke up and said something pretty daft to earn that reaction from Margaret!

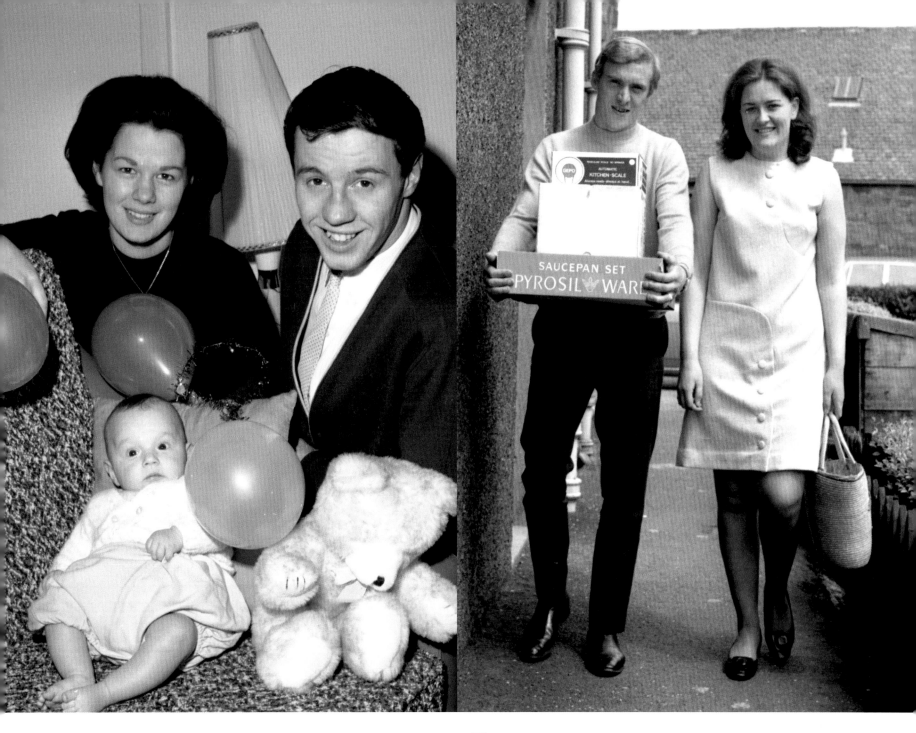

■ Willie Henderson with wife Veronica and newborn John in 1963.

■ Colin Stein moves into his new house, with wife Linda and wedding presents in 1968.

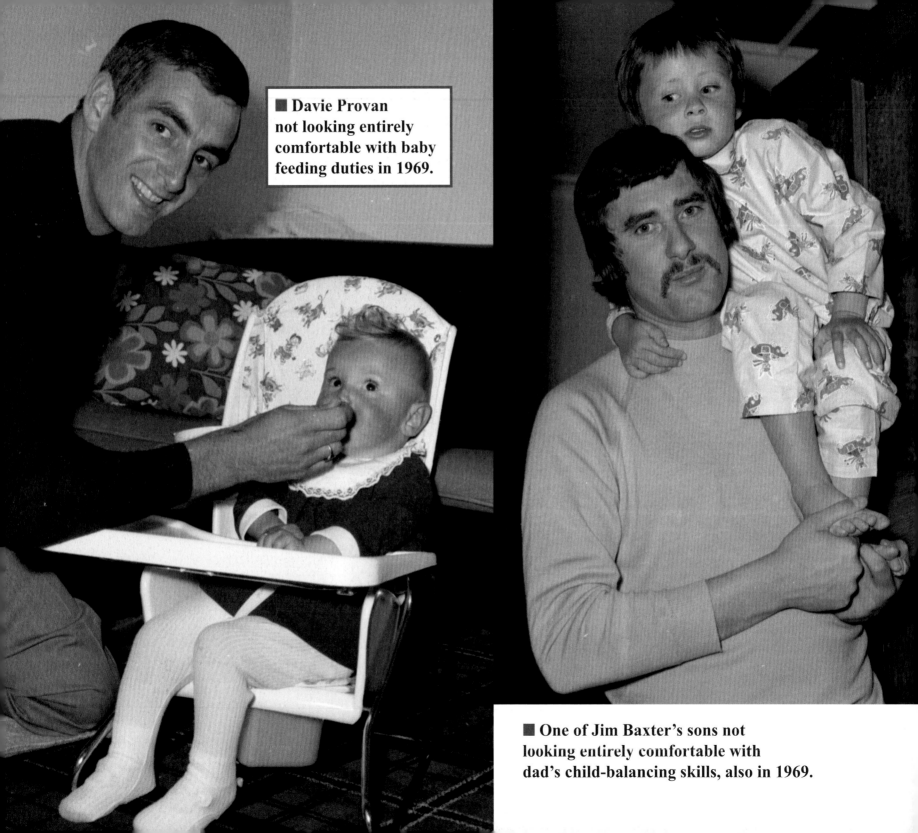

■ Davie Provan not looking entirely comfortable with baby feeding duties in 1969.

■ One of Jim Baxter's sons not looking entirely comfortable with dad's child-balancing skills, also in 1969.

■ Norrie Martin putting those big goalie hands to good use in 1964. He ran a hotel in Prestwick with his father, a former Grade 1 referee.

■ Derek Johnstone with mum Emily in 1972, and (right), a year later with his Rangers-supporting family.

■ Right: Halloween 1963, Jim Baxter chose 12-year-old Isobel Cockburn, of Ledaig Street, Glasgow, as the winner of this fancy dress competition.

■ Bobby Shearer bought a couple of ponies for his daughters, Sandra and Alison. Bobby would get up to feed, exercise and brush the ponies, Prince and Peggy, that he kept on a farm near Hamilton, before heading to training.

He is pictured with Sandra (then aged 8) and wife Helen in November 1963.

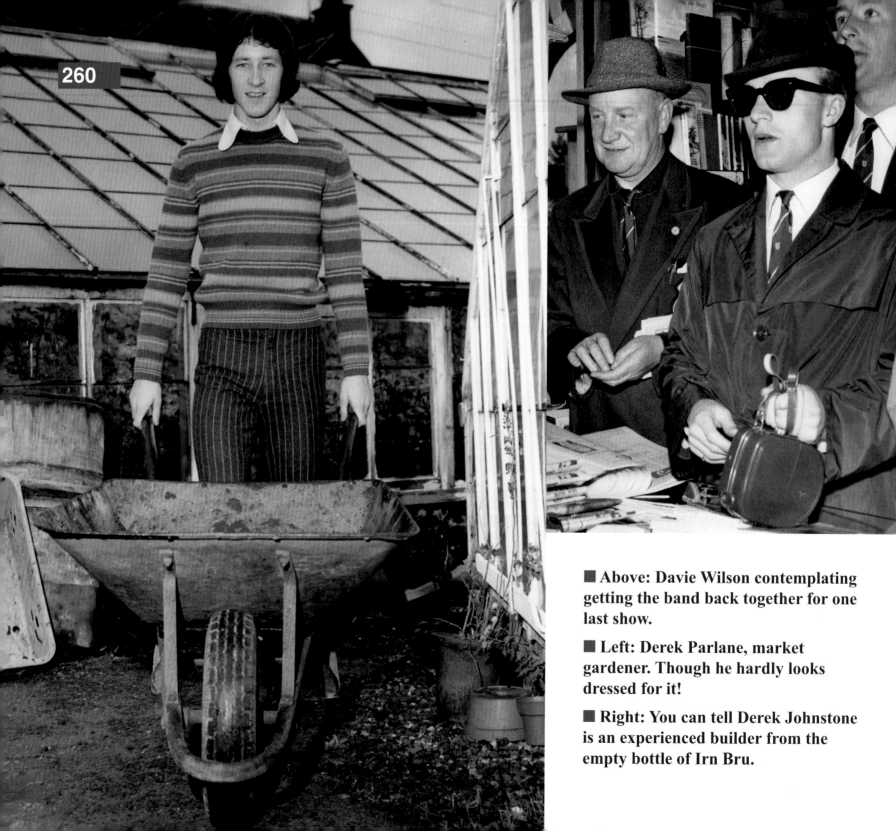

■ Above: Davie Wilson contemplating getting the band back together for one last show.

■ Left: Derek Parlane, market gardener. Though he hardly looks dressed for it!

■ Right: You can tell Derek Johnstone is an experienced builder from the empty bottle of Irn Bru.

■ Left: Avril and Davie Wilson's wedding in November 1965. And (above) Bobby Shearer, the best man.

■ **Above:** George Niven getting married to Agnes Smith in Dunfermline, in 1958, complete with battle scars (a hazard of being a 1950s goalkeeper).

■ **Right:** Harold Davis and Violet Chalmers got married in Perth in 1957.

■ Left: Derek Johnstone married computer supervisor Marian Wilson at Renfrew Parish Church in July 1978. Hundreds of well-wishers gathered outside, forcing police to control the traffic as they headed to their reception in the Eurocrest Hotel, Erskine.

■ Right: George McLean and his fiancee, model Liz Clelland, at Prestwick Airport in 1967.

■ **Alec Scott, the true blue winger who got away, with wife Annette and poodle.**

The athletic and gifted Alec was at Rangers from 1954 to '63 and was a great favourite of the blue heaven regulars with his devastating pace and shooting power. What a player he was.

He was sold to Everton for the enormous fee (at the time) of £39,000, and carried on his great form and winning habit down south.

It's a great pity that a way wasn't found to accommodate Scott and the emerging Willie Henderson in that tremendous Rangers team of the early 1960s.

■ Eric Caldow casts an eye over a painting that hung in his pub – The Eric Caldow Bar – in Hamilton. The painting (done by a pub regular) depicts his famous penalty against England that clinched the 1962 British Home Championships title.

■ **Willie Johnston, Rangers 1964-73 and 1980-82. A truly wonderful entertainer who could beat any defender and fired pin-point crosses into the box . . . and who was always quick to let referees know where they'd gone wrong.**

Rangers men

IN many ways, Ibrox has been a harsh environment for any football player over the years.

The relentless pursuit of success that is ingrained in the club means there is, to a degree, an absence of sentimentality.

There are many instances of celebrated players who have been allowed to leave when their best days are behind them, or even when they begin to show a small decline in standards. They play out their swansong years at a lesser club, no matter how good a career they enjoyed at the big house.

There is no room for passengers in a Rangers team. The best team isn't the one that won trophies in the past, it is the one that is capable of winning trophies now.

Rangers people understand this. It is a part of being the most successful club in the nation. It is indeed a harsh environment, but this is how it has to be.

So for a player to have a long career at Ibrox, to perhaps become a Rangers man – that is, a player who when his name is mentioned, people instantly think, "...of Rangers." – is a fairly unusual thing.

To be a long-serving Rangers man demands an elite standard of performance being maintained over many years. One or two bad games might be allowed, but one or two seasons of sub-standard play cannot be tolerated.

Many of the players featured in this chapter had that sort of lengthy Rangers career, or left a memorable mark on the club in some other way. These men were loyal and Ready. They possessed a physical and mental robustness above the common run of football player, or displayed skills that were truly remarkable.

In all cases, they were men able to cope with demands that players at other clubs did not have to live with. They are rewarded for their endeavours by being given immortality. They will be remembered with pride.

Men who played hundreds of games, like Eric Caldow, Willie Thornton, and Bobby Shearer.

To become a Rangers man of this stature is one of the most difficult things to achieve in Scottish football.

However, some of the players in this chapter didn't stay long, some had but fleeting careers at Ibrox and aren't well-known names: Albert Franks, Brian Heron, Reuben Evans, for instance. But they are Rangers men of a sort. But they played their part in the long story, even if it was just to put pressure on those in the first team.

Some, like former chairman John Lawrence, weren't players at all. But they were instrumental in keeping the world's most successful club continually among the football elite.

■ **Willie Thornton. A Rangers player 1936-54. A very popular figure with the crowd, Willie was one of the best headers of a ball Ibrox has ever seen.**

■ One of the reasons Rangers failed to beat Berwick in 1967 was Willie Johnston's broken leg. He is seen here being helped into hospital after the game.

■ Norrie Martin, Rangers 1958-70. Terribly unlucky with injuries, Norrie spent a lot of time in the reserves and is seen here with Second Eleven Cup after beating Hearts at Tynecastle in 1968.

■ Norrie again, showing the battle scars that could be accumulated by goalkeepers in the 1960s.

■ Willie Henderson showing the good things in life that could be accumulated by footballers in the 1960s.

■ Willie Waddell, a Rangers player 1946-56, leaves everyone, including his own team-mates, floundering in his wake. He was a devastatingly fast and powerful outside-right.

■ Willie in 1976,
turning out in a
veterans' game. He was
club manager, general
manager, consultant,
and director, 1969-92.

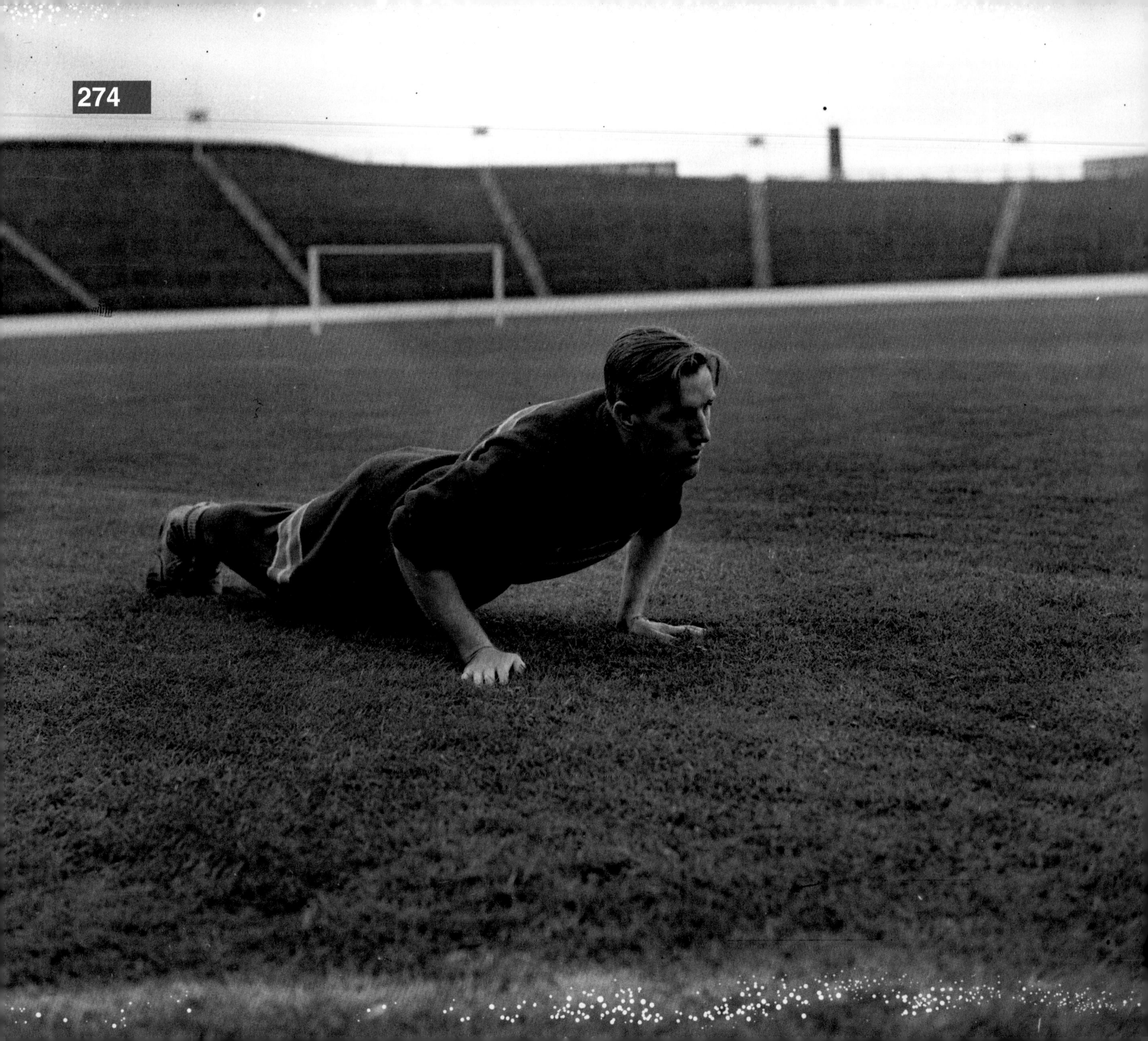

274

■ **The utterly fearless Billy Simpson, Rangers 1950-59, training at Ibrox.**

The negatives are slightly light-damaged, as many of the older ones are.

But nothing could detract from the reputation of centre-forward Billy, a Northern Irishman who was one of the great goalscorers of the post-war era.

Billy scored 163 goals for Rangers in 239 games, and a further five international goals.

He was a club record purchase, at £11,500, from Linfield, and was, like Thornton, a gifted header of a ball. Billy threw himself at crosses with incredible bravery in an era when putting your head in where the boots were flying was an extremely risky business.

Another outstanding Rangers man.

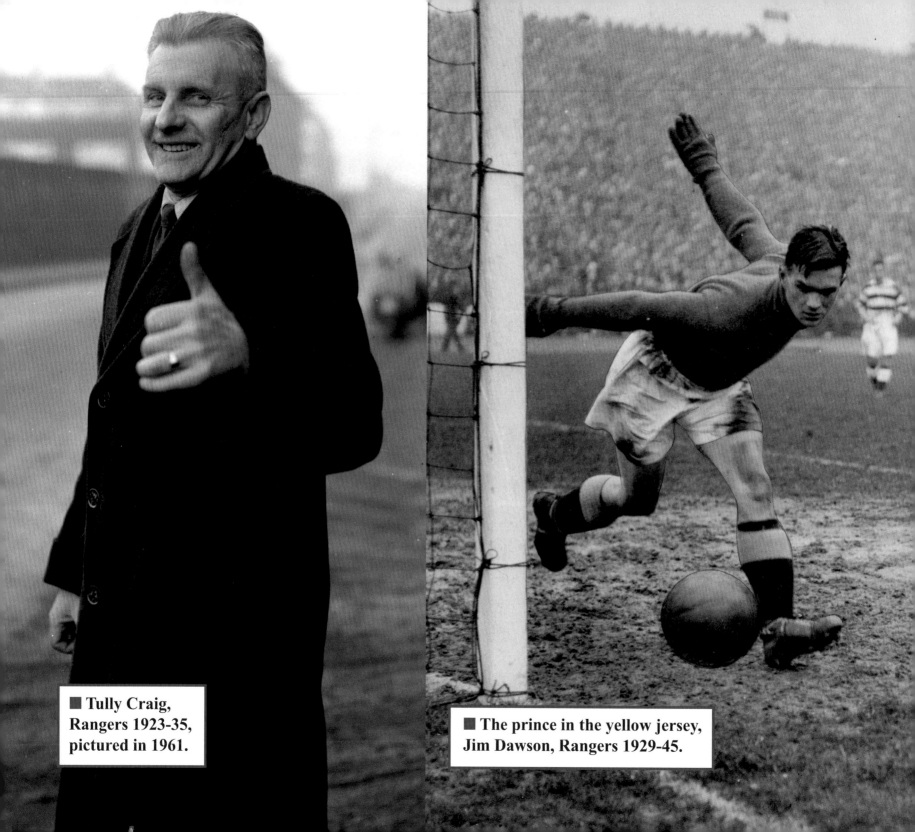

■ Tully Craig,
Rangers 1923-35,
pictured in 1961.

■ The prince in the yellow jersey,
Jim Dawson, Rangers 1929-45.

■ Billy Williamson (left) Rangers 1941-51, and Scot Symon, a Rangers player 1938-47.

■ From left – Joe Johnson (Rangers 1947-52), Willie Woodburn (1946-54), Jimmy Smith (1928-46), and Jimmy Duncanson (1946-50).

■ Bobby Shearer, Rangers 1955-65.
One of the great Rangers captains.

■ Derek Trail (Rangers 1963-66) at the Ibrox Gates.

■ Ralph Brand (Rangers 1954-65). He guaranteed goals.

■ **Tommy Muirhead (on the left) showed Carl Hansen around Glasgow, and explained the quaint local customs, on the occasion of The Great Little Dane's first Hogmanay in Scotland, in 1921.**

Hansen returned to Denmark in 1925, after his broken leg, but had to serve a two-year suspension before amateur status was granted again, allowing him to play another season for Boldklubben. He refereed league games during this suspension.

During the war, the 45-year-old Hansen was arrested by the Gestapo for shouting abuse at a Danish collaborator. He was badly beaten, and spent two months in jail, then a further two months in a concentration camp. He lost four stones during this ordeal and his health was never the same again.

He became coach of the national team for the 1952 Olympics and was a popular figure in his homeland. He managed three different clubs to win the championship.

Carl retained close links with Rangers all his life, travelling to Ibrox many times.

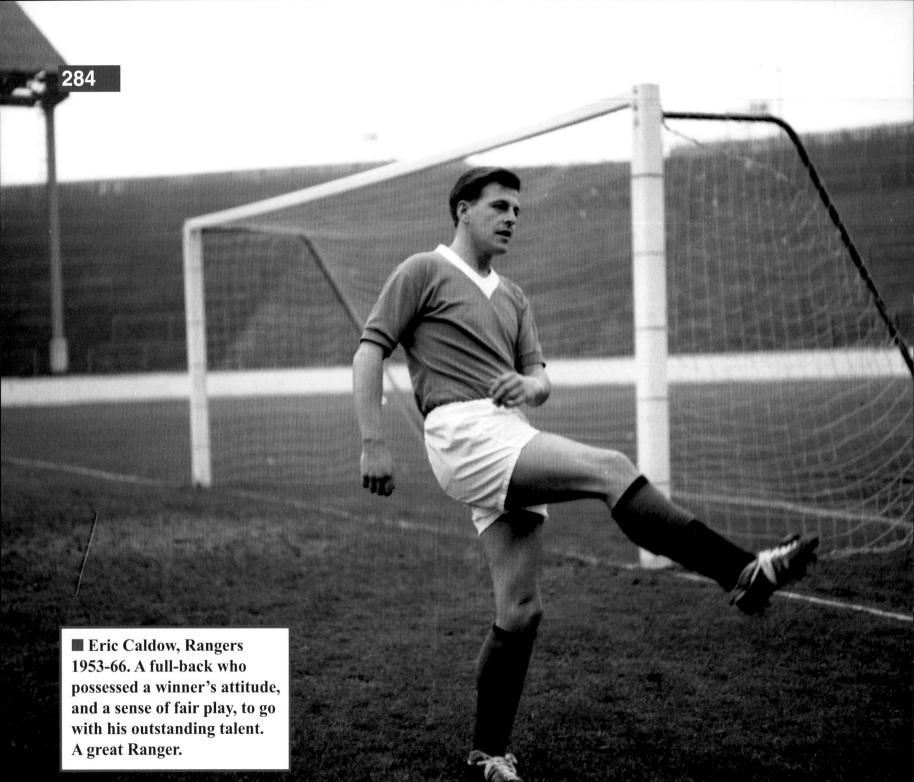

■ Eric Caldow, Rangers
1953-66. A full-back who
possessed a winner's attitude,
and a sense of fair play, to go
with his outstanding talent.
A great Ranger.

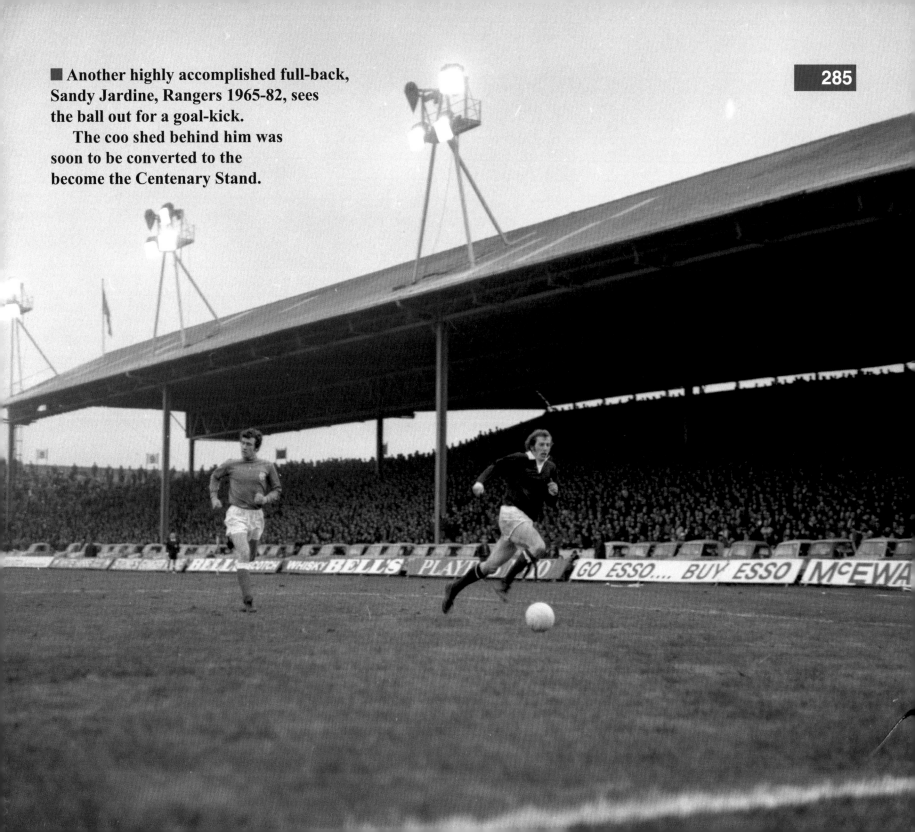

■ Another highly accomplished full-back, Sandy Jardine, Rangers 1965-82, sees the ball out for a goal-kick.

The coo shed behind him was soon to be converted to the become the Centenary Stand.

■ Left: Tommy McLean, Rangers 1971-82, and, above, Alex MacDonald, 1968-80. Men of similar stature but different demeanours. Doddie was a warrior, always 100% committed to the cause. Tommy was precise, clever, and very accurate – nowadays his "assists stats" would attract attention from all over the football world, because Tommy created wins.

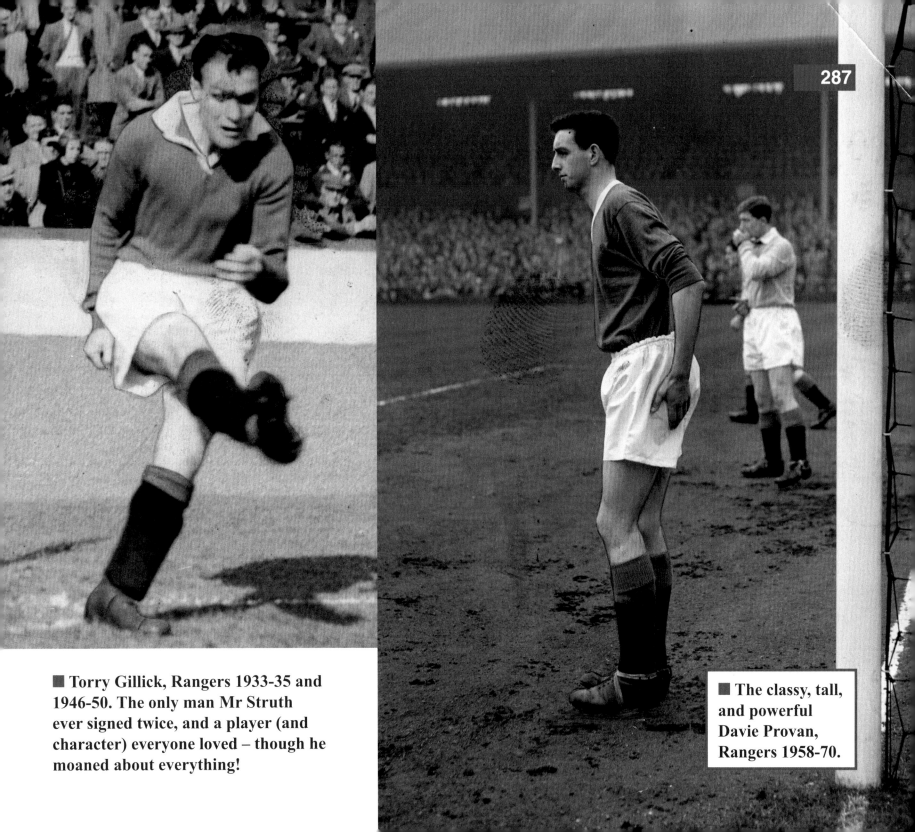

■ Torry Gillick, Rangers 1933-35 and 1946-50. The only man Mr Struth ever signed twice, and a player (and character) everyone loved – though he moaned about everything!

■ The classy, tall, and powerful Davie Provan, Rangers 1958-70.

■ Davie Wilson, Rangers 1956-67.

■ Jimmy Millar, Rangers 1955-67, partially hidden by Ron Yeats, gets one of the many goal-scoring headers of his illustrious career.

■ Billy Stevenson,
Rangers 1958-62.

■ Orjan Persson,
Rangers 1967-70.

■ **Davie Meiklejohn,
Rangers 1919-36.**

This is what a real, true blue Rangers man looks like. A winner, a born leader, a hero, a legend.

"Meek" was a one-club man, playing 563 games for Rangers. He won 12 Scottish League Championship medals and five Scottish Cup medals.

In the 1928 Scottish Cup Final, Rangers were becoming fixated with a so-called hoodoo as they hadn't won the cup for quarter of a century, despite many near misses. The game was 0-0 at half-time. Rangers were awarded a penalty and, far from this being a relief it ratcheted up the tension even more. Up stepped Davie to ram the ball home from the spot.

Rangers went on to beat Celtic 4-0 that day and complete the club's first ever Double.

■ Don Kitchenbrand, Rangers 1955-58. Never subtle, 'The Rhino' was quite a handful for defenders.

■ Johnny Hubbard, Rangers 1949-59. The frail-looking South African was a darling of the Ibrox crowd, who always take skilled wingers to their hearts. He was also another in a long line of penalty-taking experts, scoring a remarkable 50 out of 57 taken.

No matter how many times they actually took the field, they were all Rangers men.

■ **Right: powerful right-half Albert Franks, reportedly the first Englishman to sign for Rangers, arrived from Newcastle in March 1960, costing £6,500 but played only three games. He retired from the game aged 29 and forged a successful career in the CID.**

■ **Far left: winger Brian Heron signed from Ballieston in 1966 and played just a few times. But he went on to have a good career with Motherwell, Dumbarton, and a couple of clubs in England.**

■ **Left above: Reuben Evans, an inside-forward, was signed by Scot Symon in February 1960, from Dublin BB, and left for Bradford City in 1962 without ever having played a game.**

■ **Left below: Full-back Bobby King signed in August 1959 from Penicuick Athletic and played just a handful of times before leaving for Southend United in the 1963 close season.**

■ Willie Mathieson,
Rangers 1964-75.

■ Billy McPhee,
Rangers 1966-70.

■ Kai Johansen, Rangers 1965-70, with his Ibrox scrapbooks.

■ Billy Semple, Rangers 1967-71.

■ Jim Forrest, Rangers 1962-67, firing one of his 145 goals (in 163 games) past Aberdeen's John (Tubby) Ogston on September 4th, 1965.

■ Ally Dawson,
Rangers 1975-87.

■ The elegant and
skilful Dave Smith,
Rangers 1966-74.

■ Andy Penman,
Rangers 1967-73.

■ One of the
all-time greats,
Sandy Jardine,
Rangers 1965-82.

■ If you take one of us on, you take all of us on. We're all Ready.

Goalkeeper Stewart Kennedy, Rangers 1973-80, lies stretched out on the Easter Road turf after a bad challenge.

And his teammates, every single one of them, pile in to remonstrate with the ref and sort out the Hibs player who made the tackle.

No challenge to a Ranger goes unmet.

But that game in 1975 was to have a happy ending. See next page.

■ **March 29th, 1975. Colin Stein, Rangers 1968-72 and 75-78, gets to a McKean cross to plant a header past Jim McArthur – the goal that earned a 1-1 draw, the clinching point to end a long Rangers wait for a championship. There were 30,000 Bears in Hibernian's ground that day, none of whom would ever forget the scenes of jubilation.**

■ **The 1973 Scottish Cup Final. Above: Alfie Conn, Rangers 1968-74, leaves Billy McNeill in his wake, streaking though the middle to get Rangers' second goal. Below: Derek Johnstone's header comes off the post, and Tam Forsyth, Rangers 1972-82, appears from nowhere to score the winner with a raking three-inch shot.**

■ February 22, 1975. Clyde 1, Rangers 2, at the old Shawfield football stadium and dog-racing track. Bobby McKean, Rangers 1974-78, gets the opener. It would end in tragedy for Bobby when he was just 25. To this day, it isn't certain whether Bobby intended to kill himself. Whatever happened, it was a dark day for The Rangers.

■ **Football is easier for some people. It just comes naturally to them. It came very easy to Davie Cooper, Rangers 1977-89. Here he is in a Scottish Cup tie in March 1978, waltzing round Killie goalie Jim Stewart, who would go on to become a team-mate at Ibrox. Rangers won the game 4-1, and a treble, that year.**

■ Bill Paterson,
Rangers 1958-62.

■ Andy Matthew,
Rangers 1958-60.

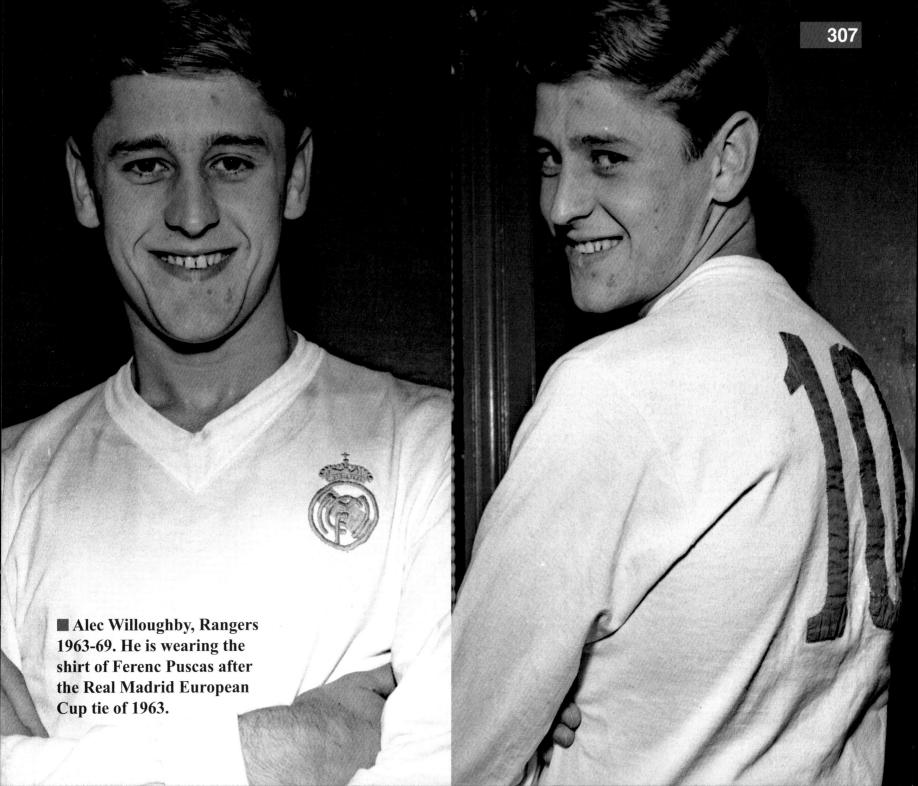

■ Alec Willoughby, Rangers 1963-69. He is wearing the shirt of Ferenc Puscas after the Real Madrid European Cup tie of 1963.

308

■ George McLean,
Rangers 1962-67,
makes the point that
surely it is acceptable
to kick Celtic players to
referee Tiny Wharton.

■ Willie Henderson, Rangers 1960-72, attempts a spectacular overhead kick in a game against Hibs in February 1971.

■ The Girvan Lighthouse, Peter McCloy, Rangers 1970-86 – one of the best Scottish goalkeepers of all time. Peter's father Jimmy was also a pro keeper.

■ Max Murray, Rangers 1955-62. Scorer of the club's first ever goal in European competition.

■ The indomitable Harold Davis, Rangers 1956-64.

■ Billy Ritchie, Rangers 1955-67. Billy was one of the first Scottish goalies to wear the large, padded gloves that are ubiquitous in modern goalkeeping. Right: Billy athletically tumbling after back-pedalling to tip a lob over the bar.

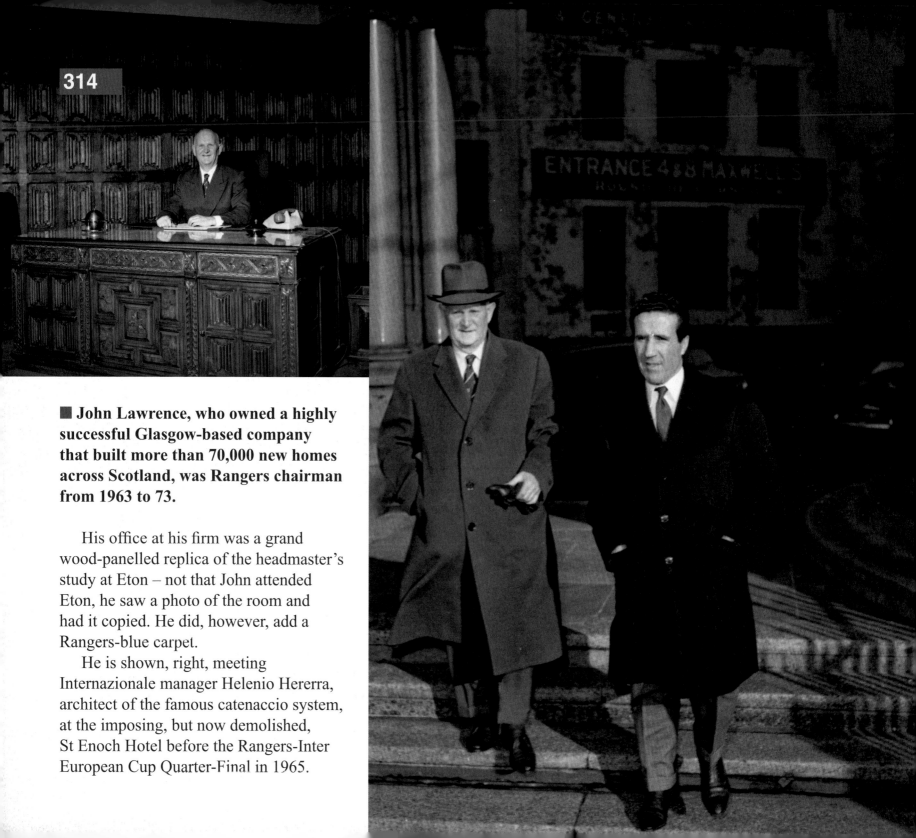

■ **John Lawrence, who owned a highly successful Glasgow-based company that built more than 70,000 new homes across Scotland, was Rangers chairman from 1963 to 73.**

His office at his firm was a grand wood-panelled replica of the headmaster's study at Eton – not that John attended Eton, he saw a photo of the room and had it copied. He did, however, add a Rangers-blue carpet.

He is shown, right, meeting Internazionale manager Helenio Hererra, architect of the famous catenaccio system, at the imposing, but now demolished, St Enoch Hotel before the Rangers-Inter European Cup Quarter-Final in 1965.

■ Derek Parlane, Rangers 1970-80. Powerful in the air and a natural goal-scorer. Derek's father Jimmy was also a Ranger just after the war.

■ Gordon Smith, Rangers 1977-80 and 82-83. Always elegant and composed, whether played in midfield or as a striker.

■ This book began with a chapter recalling the days of the Iron Curtain. All the great Rangers teams were founded upon a strong defence. If anything can be learned today from the Rangers teams of the black and white era, it is that games, and therefore titles, are won by a Young, Woodburn, McKinnon, or Greig at the back, who let the Baxters, Hendersons, and McLeans win the game further up the park. It is a tradition that has always been valued at Ibrox. Titles are Rangers' business. Victories – week in, week out – are required to achieve this.

■ The safe hands of George Niven . . .

. . . and steely centre-half play of Willie Woodburn made a solid defensive unit.

Rangers remain Rangers

THE way newspapers were made changed in the early 1980s so that they could carry colour images. The black and white era had passed, the colour era, then the digital era, came in. And the game changed with the times. New formats for old competitions, new borders to cross, new opponents to face. It must always be so.

But Rangers remain Rangers.

The names in the boardroom change, the voices shouting instructions from the dugout and on the pitch change. New heroes rise and old heroes fade away. A football club is always in a state of flux. Influential people come and go, great players come and go.

But Rangers remain Rangers.

Ibrox has changed too over the years. The terraces have disappeared, the stands have changed and then changed again. The facilities change, even the streets around the ground change.

But Rangers remain Rangers.

The fans change. Your great-grandfather stood in the old bowl-like Ibrox, you remember him as you sit in the modern stadium. Your grandchildren will sit in the Ibrox of tomorrow. Hopefully they will remember you.

Their experiences will not be the sways of packed-in crowds. It might be even more of a sanitised and static experience than it is today, if that's possible.

But Rangers will remain Rangers.

One day, another book (or collection of holograms!) will be produced recalling the Rangers of the good old days, the great players, the trophies that were won in the 2020s and 2030s.

And even then, Rangers will remain Rangers.

This book has not been a definitive history of Rangers, it has not pretended to be. It is a collection of moments and photographs of people caught in time, a reminder of great names, great games, and great times.

It only comes as far as the early 1980s, before Rangers changed Scottish football for ever with the appointment of Graeme Souness. There are many great photos from that era, but they will require another book.

In the meantime, smile, allow yourself a little nostalgia, a little longing for the old days, as you remember . . .

RANGERS
IN THE BLACK & WHITE ERA